#SAVVY

BUSINESS

OWNER

a book for small business owners

by

SAVY

IN MEMORY OF

Princess Allee,
the inspiration for
The Furever Home Friends.

2006-2019

MORE BOOKS BY SAVY

The Furever Home Friends series:

Princess Allee

Smile, Chewie!

Just Me, Wrigley

Kringle's Christmas

The Love of Senior Dogs (COMING SOON!)

Novels:

One Final Vinyl

Sculpt Yourself

The Making of a Small-Town Beauty King

90s Kids (COMING SOON!)

CONTENTS

Part 4: The Scary World of Social Media

Part 5: The Myths of Boss Babe Life

CONCLUSION
ACKNOWLEDGMENTS

INTRODUCTION

I want to address two things before this book gets going.

First, I *know* that I spelled my name wrong in the title. My name is Savy, and this book is called #SavvyBusinessOwner. I know there's an extra V in there. That's not a typo. I will address why I made this choice in Chapter 15, so you will have to be patient.

Second, I'm going to give a quick disclaimer. And this is *really* important, so please listen carefully:

This book is not going to motivate you.

This book is not going to help you believe in yourself.

This book is not going to cheer you on as you follow your dreams.

Don't get me wrong; this book isn't going to *de*-motivate you, either. I'm not here to insult you or anything like that. But my point is, if you've picked up this book, I'm assuming you *already* believe in yourself. I'm assuming that you, my reader, are already motivated to start your own business, and that you're already pursuing your dreams.

That's one of the reasons I chose to write this book: I thought the market of business self-help books needed something that went beyond basic motivation tactics and vague pieces of advice that are targeted at everyone. Actually, I think that's a major part of the problem: too many entrepreneurship books want to appeal to *everyone*—but one of the basic tenets of business theory is that you need to find your *target audience*. No product is for everyone, so why should self-help books pretend to be?

So, who's my target audience for this book? Creative people. Artists. Innovators. Self-starters. And most of all, people who are already motivated. People who *already* know that they're capable of great things, but don't know what specific steps other business owners took to bring their ideas to life. If you need me, a stranger you likely found on the internet, to tell you that *you can do it*, then in my opinion, you're not ready to start a business.

My target audience for this book is *not*: people who want to get rich quick. I am not rich. I make a below-average income. When I started writing this, someone asked, "Are you sure you're qualified to write this book? Has your business reached a high enough level of success yet?"

To that, I just yelled, "Free speech, motherf'er!" and continued writing. If you want me to tell you how to get rich off of your passion, then leave. I don't know how to get rich. I'm not going to be a millionaire before I'm 30, no matter how many entrepreneurship bots on Instagram want to pretend I can.

But what I have done is create a career. I built a business from the ground up, starting with a concept and a passion for writing and helping dogs. I am a *small* business owner, not the CEO of a major corporation.

So, if you are already the CEO of a major corporation, then you are likely not my target audience, either, since you probably know way more about business than I do.

Also, if you are part of a multi-level marketing company … I won't go so far as to say you're *not* part of my target audience, but just know that this book is *very* anti-MLM. If anything, I hope you'll read on so that I can present you some reasons why you should quit that company and start your *own* business. None of the advice in this book is meant to be applied in a multi-level marketing company, and I will elaborate further on why in Chapter 3. Though, I'll bet some of you found out about me through my anti-MLM videos on YouTube, so that shouldn't be too much of a concern.

In this book, I am aiming to be as specific as possible in each piece of advice I give. I am aiming *so hard* to be specific, that if there are any pieces of advice you're unclear on, I encourage you to contact me after reading this book for more information. On Twitter I'm @savyleiser. Send me a direct message. Or email me at savyleiser@gmail.com. My point is, I want you to feel that you got the most specific advice I could possibly give you.

I was getting *so, so tired* of business self-help books—*especially* those aimed at women—being filled with feel-good stories and vague pieces of advice that are little more than glorified common sense.

In one book I read, I was told to *invest in myself*. This author explained that she invested in herself by choosing to go to a $2,000 business seminar. She said that she absolutely did not have $2,000 available at this time, but she still paid to go to the seminar because she knew how important it was to *invest in herself*. I'm sorry, what? How do you spend $2,000 that you don't have? Where did the money physically come from? Did you write a faulty check? Max out your credit cards? Get a loan? If you got a business loan, *how* did you get it? What was the application process like? What documents did the bank require? How did you get approved when you had so little in your account? Did you take up drug-dealing for a few weekends? Did you steal the money? Or did you have $2,000 already, but just said you didn't so you'd sound more relatable to the rest of us?

Other books have told me that I have to eat healthy, exercise, and stay skinny in order to be a successful business owner, since keeping commitments to your business starts with keeping diet commitments to yourself. Sorry, but that's straight-up BS. I spend way more hours in a day on my business than on my appearance, and that's just how it goes. I have my own set of priorities, and ever since I overcame an OCD-induced eating disorder about a decade ago and subsequently got medication, being skinny has no longer been one of them.

Most books I've read aimed at female business owners talk a lot about what it's like to balance running a business while raising kids. I'll have to let you guys know something upfront: I don't have kids. I'm a dog mom, and that's likely all I'll ever be. Chewie's a nuisance, but he's also the best goshdarn business partner I've ever had. That's not to say that this book isn't for you if you have kids: it still is! I just mean that I won't have any specific advice to give about balancing mom life with boss life, because I've never had to do that. But luckily for you, the market is already flooded with books about that very topic, so you're good to go! I'd actually recommend checking out Sheryl Sandberg's *Lean In* if you want to learn more about that specific topic; I personally did not find the book useful since

I'm not a mother myself, but it was full of amazing advice for working moms.

What *none* of these books have told me is *how* to start a business. How does one raise startup capital? Do you have to start off rich? Should you pursue venture capitalists? Should you take out a loan? What basic concepts and terms does a regular person with no formal business education need to know? What goes into an online store, versus a brick and mortar store, versus Etsy or Amazon? How much does it cost to run an office? To manage employees? Is it better to hire full-time employees, contract workers, or to do everything yourself?

Don't get me wrong; I don't have definitive answers to all these points. But I am going to talk about my thought process for all these concepts and share my experiences with them, both good and bad.

I guess you could say, "I'm not like other #bossbabes. I'm a #savvybusinessowner."

PART 1

Becoming an Entrepreneur:
The Anecdotal Stuff

1

A Portrait of the Artist as a Young Nerd

The first fan-letter I ever wrote was to Pleasant Rowland, founder of Pleasant Company, which produced the American Girl dolls and books until Mattel bought them out at the end of the 90s. Now, my memory on *when* exactly I wrote this letter is a little hazy; I vaguely remember being eight years old, but that would've been in 2000, which was after the Mattel buyout. Either way, the contents of the letter are still clear in my mind: I wanted to know *why* Pleasant Company wasn't publicly traded. *Why* couldn't I find them when I scanned the New York Stock Exchange in the Sunday newspaper? As a fan of the American Girl dolls and books, the next logical step in my mind was to buy stock in the company.

Now, in the 90s, I grew up in a low-income household. It's not like I had thousands of dollars available as a child to buy stock in a company. I could barely afford their dolls; I saved up a *lot* of garage sale money to get Molly from World War II. But my thought process at the time was: if you like something, buy stock in it. Anything you enjoy, you should become a part of.

My childhood stock-trading phase is probably one of the weirder things about me, and that's saying a lot, considering I spent the entirety of my high-school years trying to channel major manic pixie dream girl energy.

Have you ever had one of those "future me will thank past me for this" moments? Like when you're super drunk and actually remember to drink water? Or when you're super drunk and decide to file IRS paperwork to officially register your LLC as a legal entity? (That one might be just me.) Well, I had one of those moments about a year ago.

I was 26 years old, about a year and a half into running The Furever Home Friends, and I was stuck. I couldn't figure out how to grow my business and scale it to the next level. Sure, I knew *what* I needed to do: I needed to get stuffed animals of all four characters produced by a manufacturer, I needed to get my books printed in bulk quantities so

I could decrease my per-unit printing costs, and I needed to start traveling to larger conventions and festivals as a vendor. But I didn't know *how* to do that. Meaning: I didn't know where I would get the *money* for it.

That is, until I remembered my weird childhood stock trading phase.

When I wanted to try out investing as a kid, my mom was adamant that I not monitor the stocks too strongly. My dad explained that stocks go up and down, and if you pull out your money just because it's in a low place at the time, you'll end up losing in the end. Maybe if you just gave that stock five or ten more years, it would've gone back up.

So, just as they suggested, I forgot about it.

Until I was 26 years old, and suddenly remembered that I *did* have money. I checked the investment account I'd set up forever ago, and I was astonished: the small Christmas and birthday checks I'd invested as a kid had increased to nearly $5,000. Not *everything* I needed to get this business to the next level, but a darn solid chunk of it. I called up the bank and arranged for the stocks to be sold and the money to be transferred to my bank account. Within a few months, my full stuffed animal line was up for sale.

That's just one of many stories about how, in a lot of ways, I feel like I've been preparing to be a business owner my whole life.

Once, one of my friends asked me if I was an author or a business owner first. We were talking about this because we were deep in an argument about which of the vlogbrothers each of us were: in this case, we were both claiming we were Hank. (Sorry, John. Although, I have a quote from one of your books tattooed on my side, so you honestly shouldn't feel bad.) My reasons for identifying with Hank were clear: I look like a blonde nerdy boy, I primarily write contemporary sci-fi speculative new-adult novels about bisexual women interacting with strange technology, and I'm a business owner first. (If none of this makes sense to you, I highly recommend checking out the vlogbrothers, John and Hank Green.) *haha*

Anyway, it's hard to tell which passion came first: writing or entrepreneurship. Sure, my five-year-old self loved to write stories wherever I could. My grandparents would staple coupons and fliers together so I could write on the back of them and pretend I was writing a "book." But I would also draw up ugly crayon diagrams of weird inventions I had, take them with to Toys R' Us, and ask to speak to the purchasing manager about getting my *LOL!* "product" on their shelves. (Yes, two decades before I had a half-shaved-head haircut, I was already asking to speak to the manager.)

In high school, I tried to start a group called the Young Entrepreneurs' Club. I had a few friends who wanted to join. I got the idea when I constantly saw other clubs, teams, and groups fundraising by selling baked goods, merch, and other items in the school lobby. I proposed the idea to a few teachers. It went like this:

Me: I want to start a new club. Will you be the faculty advisor?

Teacher: What's the club?

Me: The Young Entrepreneurs' Club.

Teacher: What does the club do?

Me: We learn about business through practical hands-on experience.

Teacher: How do you do that?

Me: Well, you know how clubs are always having bake sales to raise money?

Teacher: Yeah.

Me: We do that. We have bake sales, maybe sell other things too, in the lobby, and we raise money.

Teacher: And then where does the money go?

Me: We keep it. We're entrepreneurs. That's the whole point.

No one approved the club.

Either way, I'm fortunate to live in a time when there's a fairly low barrier to entry to becoming both an author *and* an entrepreneur. The first time I tried to combine these two passions was middle school. In study hall, friends would talk to me about how they "liked some guy/girl" and "didn't know how to tell them." So I'd ask them to

Love This! *There's a story here*

give me a list of reasons they liked them, and then I'd write out a full harlequin-romance-style love letter they could give to the other person.

No one ever actually paid me for this service. In fact, most people begged me *not* to give the love letter to their crush. I guess this was my first introduction to the idea of a *target audience*, as well as *supply and demand*. There was no demand for hyper-romanticized love letters, at least not among the target audience of awkward middle schoolers. Imagine my shock.

Though these various failed business ventures are fun to look back on and laugh, none of them were true business experiences. I didn't fully understand what entrepreneur life was like until I started The Furever Home Friends in 2017 at age 24. And let me tell you: the reality of entrepreneur life, along with the insane sacrifices you'll have to make, punched me right in the face.

Before we get into all the specifics of what I learned each step of the way, which I will delve into deeply in later chapters, I will give you all a brief overview of how I started The Furever Home Friends and what my business represents.

When I was 14 years old, my family adopted a beautiful Black Labrador named Allee from a shelter in Pennsylvania. We named her after my two recently deceased grandfathers: my mom's father, Al, and my dad's father, Lee. Pretty soon, my mom started calling her "Princess Allee" and "Diva Dog" because of how much she loved to demand attention from people. She was a very well behaved puppy, but whenever someone other than her was getting attention, she'd do a strange bark-howl combination in the back of her throat until someone turned around to pet her and tell her how pretty she was.

Over the years, my mom would tell me, "You need to write a book about Princess Allee, the Diva Dog." And I did; I wrote a few drafts of different books about Allee over my high school years.

In September of 2016, I was 24 years old, working as a music journalist, and spending every possible second writing novels, building a social media presence as an author, and trying to get my writing career off the ground. In the middle of working on quirky YA novels, I would frequently come back to my drafts of *Princess Allee*, my picture book about a black lab who just wanted to be a princess. Shortly after I adopted my dog, Chewie, it all came together for me: this could be a series.

One of the first things that my husband, Tyler, and I learned about Chewie before adopting him was that he had been previously shot in the face. His face and ears had at least nine pellets embedded under his fur, likely from a birdshot incident. His wounds had healed before the shelter took him in, and the vet saw no need to make additional incisions since he never noticed that the pellets were still in his face. Another thing, however, quickly became clear: Chewie had severe anxiety. He struggled to meet new dogs. He struggled during thunderstorms and fireworks (but then again, what dog doesn't?). He struggled when we tried to leave him home so we could go to work.

I had anxiety too. This was also right around the time that I first started getting medicated for my OCD. I suddenly realized: dogs have *a lot* in common with us. We all go through difficult situations that influence our outlooks going forward. And there was a lesson here for kids.

Soon, I started writing drafts of a potential book about Chewie as well.

By the end of my first draft of *Smile, Chewie!*, it was clear to me that this was *not* a traditional book series. Or at least, I didn't want it to be. I had no desire to pitch these books to an agent or to secure a book deal. I wanted Furever Home Friends to be its own complete business.

This would be how I could combine all of my passions: writing, toys, dogs, and, of course, entrepreneurship.

Once I conceived of this book series, I drew some inspiration from my 90s idol, Pleasant Rowland. When books and toys work *together*, kids can really learn a lot and connect strongly with a character on an emotional level. My love for my

American Girl doll, Molly from 1944, got me excited to read books about World War II and learn all about history. My dogs had the potential to do this as well. A book *and* a stuffed animal about each featured dog could create a forever beloved character. (Plus, anyone who knows me knows that I love toys *way* too much. Even as an adult.)

I also took some inspiration from Build-A-Bear. I actually remember when Build-A-Bear was first founded; it was in 1997, when I was five years old. My mom told me about this amazing cool new place you could go to build, name, and "adopt" your own new stuffed animal friend, and I was hyped beyond belief. One of the things I loved most about Build-A-Bear as a kid were the adoption certificates you could make at the end. You could name your bear, make it clear that they belonged to you, indicate the date, and more.

As I was building the Furever Home Friends, I was well aware that, because I was incorporating the book-and-toy model like American Girl, and I was offering adoption certificates like Build-A-Bear, that these companies would be my competitors. For me, identifying my competitors early on was helpful not only to figure out how I'd be different, but also to gain inspiration from what they were doing well.

Looking at these elements helped me nail down my business's *mission* and *purpose*. Sure, I was writing books about dogs. But *why*? I wanted to create stuffed animals that matched these dogs. But *why*? I wanted to include customized adoption certificates in every order, and I wanted to donate a portion of profits to no-kill animal shelters. But *why*?

It could be easy to say, "Well, because I love dogs!" or, "Because I love writing!" But I'm not my own target customer. And dogs aren't my customers, either; they don't even have money! (Silly dogs.) My target *audience* was kids, which meant my target *customers* were parents. So, my business's mission had to center on how my work could benefit *them*. I eventually came up with the following mission statement:

Sharing real dogs' stories
Teaching kids about social issues
Helping dogs in need
Making friends furever

This statement represented what my business did (shared dogs' stories) and what the target audience would take away from it (teaching kids about social issues). When it came down to it, my business was all about spreading social awareness through beloved characters that kids could emotionally and empathetically connect with. That's a good mission for parents and teachers (the target customer), because parents and teachers want something that's both fun and educational for their kids.

At the time I'm writing this, I'm 27 years old. (My goal is to release this book on my 28th birthday; let's see if this sentence makes it into the final draft!) I've been running the Furever Home Friends for over two years, and in that time, I've learned so much about what makes a business grow.

At the same time, I know that I'm still young and that my business will grow a lot more as I do. I'm so excited to take you all on this journey with me.

2

Creativity + Business

When I was in high school, my guidance counselor asked if I was more of a "math and science" person or a "history and English" kind of person. I told her I was actually a "math and English" person, and she looked at me like I had three heads, then told me that wasn't possible, and I had to pick one of the other two. I guess back in the late 2000s, we were all still subscribing to the pedagogical theory that students were either predominantly right or left brained. I'm not entirely sure if that's been debunked or not, but I'll tell you my personal opinion: like many things in life, it's BS.

During my time in grad school at DePaul, one of the business school professors introduced me to a colleague as, "One of our business students." I then told her that I was an English major. But it was a reasonable misunderstanding; even as an English major, getting my Master's in Writing & Publishing, I spent the majority of my time in the business school building, going to panels and talks, entering competitions, and soaking up as much knowledge from the people around me who actually *did* go to business school.

You might be asking, "Savy, why didn't you go to business school? Why were you getting an English Master's instead, especially if you were trying to run a business?"

The answer is simple: money.

I got a graduate assistantship in the English department and got all my tuition waived. I did not get a tuition waiver for business school. Yet, I could still take advantage of many of their resources just from being a student of the university. The choice was obvious.

2017 was a crazy year for me. Toward the beginning of the year, I applied to grad school for a Master's in Writing & Publishing. I applied to get a graduate assistantship so all my tuition could be waived; if I didn't get the assistantship, I wasn't going to go to grad school at all. As this was also the year I was starting up the Furever Home Friends, I knew I could not afford to take on *any* loans or debt.

I was excited to get my acceptance letter to my chosen graduate program; however, a few weeks later, I was disappointed to learn that all graduate assistantship roles had already been filled, and I was going to be put on a waitlist. Because it was unlikely I'd get the tuition waived, I decided not to go to grad school. Instead, I went ahead full force on building my business and planning my wedding.

August 11, 2017 was *the craziest* day of my life, and I mean that in the best possible way. It was the release date of the first two books in the Furever Home Friends series, *Princess Allee* and *Smile, Chewie!* It was also exactly seven weeks until my wedding.

It was *also* the day that, in between doing tons of social media promotions to celebrate my new "book birthday," I received an email that I wasn't expecting.

A spot had opened up in the graduate assistantship program. I could go to school for free. And I'd start in a month.

In September of 2017, I started my Master's program, I turned 25, I got married, *and* I had just started a new business. Between going to class, working 20 hours a week on grad assistant work to waive my tuition, publicizing my own books and trying to grow my business, *plus* teaching kids' creative writing workshops and writing magazine articles about music (because, believe me, the Furever Home Friends was strongly *revenue negative* at the beginning), I worked about 90-95 hours a week. I didn't take my honeymoon until July of 2019, nearly two years after the wedding itself. I made the sacrifices I needed to—and as a result, September 2017 is one of the months I look back on most fondly.

When I started attending business school events and getting business coaching at DePaul, someone gave me some great advice: "If you can go to school for free, *always* do it. I don't care if you're eight months pregnant; if an opportunity comes up to get an education for free, *get that education*." This was from a woman who worked at the business school and *also* worked around 90 hours a week, just like I did. She knew I had made the right choice.

I ended up spending my two years in grad school studying creativity and entrepreneurship at the same time, but in vastly different ways. My classes were largely creative; as a Writing & Publishing major, I took classes about book publicity, copyediting, creative writing, and more. But when I wasn't in class, I went to business talks. I went to coaching sessions to learn about maximizing revenue, developing marketing strategies, and balancing finances.

Through all of this, I realized that the way I had interpreted myself in high school had been right all along: I wasn't a right-brained or left-brained person. I wasn't a STEM person or a humanities person. I was a creative businessperson. I was a person who loved every part of building my business—the creativity of writing my books and designing my own covers, the logistics of tracking expenses in a spreadsheet, the satisfaction of a productive strategizing session. It didn't matter if what I was doing was creative or mathematical in nature; I loved *all* of it, and I knew I wouldn't want to do a job where I'd have to commit to one or the other. For me, that's what helped me feel confident in my decision not to be a traditional author.

When I was an undergrad in college, I loved to take screenwriting classes. I had one professor who would frequently talk about how, once inside the film industry, screenwriters must face the difficulty of having to consider marketability and the commercial appeal of their work. It wasn't all about the purity of a story well told; it was about what people wanted to *buy*. That made perfect sense to me; I wasn't even sure why we were discussing it. Instead, I was the kid constantly raising my hand to ask, "Okay, but when are we going to talk about the *business* side of screenwriting? When I finish this script, what are the concrete next steps I need to take for this to get produced? How do I secure funding? How do I pitch to studios versus indie filmmakers?" I never got the answers to these questions; instead I was told that, for the purpose of the class, I should just focus on the content of the story.

So I did that. I wrote a script I was damn proud of. I got an A in the class. And then I went to pitch the script to agents, managers, and entertainment lawyers. And I learned that having a plot that relies on Beatles music is a *terrible idea* and *copyright infringement* and a *legal nightmare*. So, that script sits in a drawer somewhere, and I sit at my desk at home, still bitter that nobody wanted to talk to me about the business side of writing when I was 20.

Bitterness aside, I passionately believe that both sides of the brain need to work together to create a successful business. Creative thinking, logistical thinking, and everything in between, are *all* necessary to bring something new into the world and maximize its reach.

Don't get me wrong; each type of thinking is wonderful and valuable on its own as well. I know plenty of fellow authors who have taken the traditional publishing route because they don't want to do as much entrepreneurial work; they want to focus all their energy on *writing*. I completely understand that! Conversely, I also have friends who work in software development, accounting, programming, and other STEM fields. These people don't want to think about using numbers and figures to tell a story; for them, the magic is in solving a problem with pure logic. I can definitely see the appeal of this as well! As Spock would say, live long and prosper, friends!

For me, though, neither type is enough on its own. I need to break up my days with different types of activities that engage different parts of the brain. I was the kid who applied to college for film and creative writing, but spent all of high school excitedly talking about my AP Physics and Calculus classes. I was the grad student who spent all my time at business school events, despite being the only English major there. Deep down, I'm still the kid arguing with my guidance counselor about how I don't have to prioritize one type of learning over another. I guess that's why I was always meant to be a business owner in a creative field.

This type of thinking — balancing the creative with the entrepreneurial — also allowed me to see the world of publishing, as well as the concept of *books* at large, in a completely new light.

As an author, I see books as a work of art. But as a business owner, I see books as a *product*. Seeing books in both ways at once has allowed me to break free of the trap that I will call the *publishing binary*.

As we've progressed deeper into the 21st century, technology has created a boom in the self-publishing industry. Concepts like print-on-demand allow independent authors to enter the game. I think this is a welcome change; however, I don't like that it has turned our thinking from a monolith (*the only way to get a book published is to pitch it to an agent and then get a book deal from a publisher*) into a binary (*the only two ways to get a book publisher are a) to pitch it to an agent and get a book deal from a publisher, or b) to self-publish it*). I like to think that there are infinite ways to get a book into the world, just as there are with any product. I don't like to think of my books as *traditionally published* or as *self-published*; I like to think of them as a key product in the larger Furever Home Friends business. My stuffed animals aren't traditionally published or self-published, either. They're a product, just like my books.

Even if you're not planning to start a book business, I still think this example can be relevant to you. Everything created in a business is a product, and every product needs to be thought of in two ways: in terms of its quality (in my case, storytelling, writing, and art quality) and in terms of its function as a good or service within the business itself.

So that's why, right here, I'm asking everyone to think *outside* of any possible binaries for your field. Books are not just traditionally published or self-published. Toys are not just handmade or mass-produced. Students are not just STEM kids or artsy kids. There are no binaries in any part of life, including business.

And now, I'm going to ask that you please don't kill me or cancel me or angrily tweet about me.

(Actually, you can if you want to; that will increase my relevance in social media algorithms!) I know I went on and on in the introduction about how I refuse to give any vague advice in this book, but I have to give just one piece: No matter what business you're going into, find ways to balance creative thinking with entrepreneurial thinking. Find ways to mix art and emotion with numbers and logistics. Find a way to make it all work together, and maybe you will also see your business concept in a new light.

Would love to talk more about this!

3

Do Not Join a Pyramid Scheme

In the past few years, one of the biggest acts of disrespect I've seen to small business owners is the linguistic appropriation of multi-level marketing companies referring to themselves as "small businesses."

I've read *way* too many business books and self-help books that make it sound like multi-level marketing (or MLM) companies are a valid way to start your own business. So, let me just get this out of the way here: that's a lie at best, and targeted manipulation at worst.

I have been an active participant in the anti-MLM movement for about three years at this point, and many of my videos on YouTube break down why MLMs are so harmful—not just to their own employees, but also to small business owners.

Let me make a few things clear before I proceed in this chapter: I have nothing against the *people* working for MLM companies. All the salespeople I've met for Tupperware or LuLaRoe or Mary Kay have been sweet, kind, and friendly people. My critique of MLMs does not have anything to do with negative feelings toward individual people; it is all about the predatory nature of the corporate entities that run these companies. I blame the structure of the companies themselves, as well as the corporate people at the top of these companies, for their manipulative practices. I do not blame the individual consultants or distributors who are likely working hard for little to no income.

This chapter might seem a little out of place since it's not about my personal business experience or my story. But I do think this chapter is important in this kind of book, because multiple business books I've read—particularly those targeted at women—have talked about direct sales or MLM companies as options for entrepreneurs. So, if you want to start your own business, if you have an entrepreneurial spirit, if you enjoy selling things, let me make my advice very clear: do *not*, under *any* circumstances, join an MLM company.

I also need to make another thing clear before someone tries to jump up my butt for slander: yes, by law, MLMs and pyramid schemes are technically different. Pyramid schemes are investment structures where you must recruit people below you to give you money, which flows to the top. An MLM sells a product, and you recruit others to sell the product under you for a cut of your commission. In both cases, you have to pay to join the company, and you earn more when you recruit others below yourself.

But in my personal experience (which, if you didn't want to hear it, why did you start reading this?), regardless of any technicalities or differences, *both* of these types of companies will rob you of your autonomy as a business owner and likely put you into debt.

Why Aren't MLMs Small Businesses?

I think this is an important distinction to draw. Many MLM companies will advertise to new recruits that you can "run your own business" or become a "small business owner." Amway refers to their distributors as "independent business owners," often shortened to IBOs.

But here's why that is dishonest: when you own your own business, *you* are in control of the products, the price points, the distribution, and more. Sure, you can hire people to take over these tasks for you, but at the end of the day, if *you* own the business, there isn't a corporation that can come in and say, "No, you can't sell that bracelet for $10; it has to be $5." When *you* own a business, no one can tell you, "You can't sell that on Amazon; you can only sell it through a company-approved website." When *you* own a business, no one can tell you, "No, you can't order 200 pairs of black leggings; you'll get whatever colors we, the manufacturers, decide to give you."

MLMs completely rob their distributors of the freedom and the choice that actual small business owners have. Now, if that kind of thing doesn't bother you — not being able to choose what the products look like or how much they cost — you can always buy a franchise. In fact, some people like to think that their MLM is similar to a franchise since they are operating an independent business selling another corporation's products. However, that's also false.

Why Aren't MLMs Franchises?

Because of sales territories.

One of the most important facets of sales is having a *territory*. If you have two of the exact same business competing at the same location, you're screwed. If you're going to become a franchisee for

McDonald's, you can't set up your restaurant right next to someone else's McDonald's. You will never be encouraged to recruit your mom and your uncle and your twelve cousins to all open their own McDonald's on your street as well.

I think the franchise model is actually how a lot of MLMs have survived; back in the 60s, 70s, and 80s, MLMs actually *did* function a lot more like franchises. A neighborhood had one Mary Kay lady and one lady that hosted Tupperware parties. These consultants didn't recruit others in the neighborhood to sell the same products, because then they'd create competition for themselves.

However, social media has completely changed the game. With MLMs allowing consultants the ability to sell their products online, ship products all over the country (or the world), connect through Instagram DMs, and sell through Facebook groups, the concept of a *sales territory* has been completely obliterated. Suddenly, it no longer mattered if you were your neighborhood's Mary Kay lady, because your neighbors could be friends with another Mary Kay lady 1,000 miles away who shipped them products purchased online. On the internet, there are no territories. As a result, these companies began pushing recruitment more than selling products directly to consumers. According to the website PinkTruth, which includes blog posts and testimonies from multiple former Mary Kay consultants, many Mary Kay representatives report making significantly more money through recruitment than through direct sales in the age of social media.

The problem with MLMs in the age of the internet is that they encourage you to recruit your own competition. Now, healthy competition is necessary in any market; there's a reason we don't want businesses turning into monopolies. But in the cases of MLMs, individual consultants are not allowed to set their own prices, choose their own products, or do anything to set themselves apart from their competition. They *are* encouraged to recruit others to join because they will get a cut of the sales commission from everyone who joins under them.

So, what happens in this case? The market becomes oversaturated. Most of us have probably heard of one of the most foundational concepts in business: supply and demand. If there is a lot of demand and not a huge supply, the products sold become more financially valuable. If there is a huge supply but no demand, the products become worthless. With no barriers to entry and no sales territories, too many people are selling the exact same product, without any increase in demand for it. The supply increases, but the demand stays the same; and as a result, nobody makes money.

Can you imagine if franchise businesses operated like MLMs? What if the corporate heads for Dunkin' Donuts started encouraging all their franchisees to recruit others to start *more* Dunkin' Donuts stores with no cap on how many they should recruit? Next thing you know, there are three or four Dunkin' Donuts stores on the same block. How can they compete, when they're the exact same brand, selling the exact same products? The result would be that all of these individual stores would make less money, while the corporate people up top continued to profit.

Why Do People Join MLMs?

But Savy, you might be saying, *if MLMs are so awful, why would people even join them in the first place?*

MLMs, like every type of business, have found a target audience and have appealed to exactly what they're looking for. Many people recruited into MLMs are low-income women and new moms. These people are often looking for a job that allows them to work from home, set their own hours, and make money to support their families.

At my time of writing this, only four US states require companies to offer paid maternity leave to full-time employees. As a result, women often get overlooked for promotions due to the risk of pregnancy. When women do get pregnant and have to take time off of work to physically heal, they often are not compensated for this time. When they go back to work, they face day-care costs in the tens of thousands. Now, none of this is a problem *on its own*; obviously, day-care centers have to make money too, and looking after kids is *hard work* (just ask any parent!).

But the problem stems from the fact that, because a lot of parents cannot afford day-care (and also can't afford to survive on just one parent's income), it becomes necessary for one parent to work from home.

But Savy, you might be saying, *this sounds exactly like me! I need a job where I can work from home!* In this case, I'd recommend looking for remote work; there are lots of customer-service jobs available where you can take calls or tickets over the phone or online. I know it's not easy, and I'd never blame anyone for being in this kind of position; as a person without kids, I am in no place to judge a parent's choices for supporting their family. However, the Federal Trade Commission has found that over 99 percent of people in MLMs make *no* money (and many of them *lose* money), so if you are a parent in this situation, just know that MLMs are *not* the way out. Most people who join MLMs hoping to make a better life for their families end up putting their families deeper into debt.

#SAVVYBUSINESSOWNER

But SAVY, you might be saying once again, *if struggling working parents are their target audience, and target audiences are used to determine the primary customer base for a product, wouldn't that make these consultants the customers of the company, rather than the employees? The MLM is the company, the 'business opportunity' is the product, and the consultants are the customers, right?*

DING DING DING! That's the biggest problem of all with the MLM business structure; if you join an MLM, you will not be a business owner, nor will you be an employee. You will get none of the freedom of a business owner and none of the benefits of being a salaried employee. Instead, you will get all the financial liability of being a *customer*. You will pay a company for the *privilege* of working for *them*. And they will be presenting this to you as an amazing work opportunity. In reality, they are advertising their own product to *you*.

How Can I Spot an MLM?

MLMs can be sneaky; sometimes they try to masquerade as direct-sales companies or franchises. Herbalife pretends that you can buy a franchise of a health club; in reality, you'll be recruited into a downline to sell supplements and other sketchy health products. (For more information about the structure of Herbalife, I highly recommend the documentary *Betting on Zero*, which — at least at the time that I'm writing this—is available to watch on Netflix.)

Here's a way to figure out what kind of company is trying to recruit you:

- If the company offers you a yearly salary or payment per hour worked, congratulations! This is a legitimate job.

- If the company offers you commission for each product you sell, but you DO NOT have to pay anything upfront to join the company, and CANNOT recruit others to sell below you, then this is a legitimate direct sales job. These are rare, and often actually *will* try to get you to recruit people once you're deeply involved in the business; be careful with these. But I won't generalize and say that *all* direct-sales jobs are bad.

- If the company makes you pay to join, but does not allow you to recruit others under you, this *might* be a franchise opportunity; again, just be cautious of these.

- If the company makes you pay to join (*regardless* of how large or small the startup fee is), pays you a commission for number of products sold, and also encourages you to recruit others, this is an MLM. Run!

- If the company prioritizes recruitment of others above selling products to external customers, this is a straight-up pyramid scheme. Run for the *hills*!

As of 2019, here are some well-known MLMs for reference. This is not a complete list, however; always do your research on any company you're planning to work with!

Avon, Mary Kay, LuLaRoe, Tupperware, Arbonne, Beachbody, Rodan + Fields, Herbalife, DoTerra Essential Oils, Perfectly Posh, JuicePlus, Young Living Essential Oils, Younique, Paparazzi Jewelry, Cocoa Exchange, Norwex, Usborne Books & More (though this company does have a legitimate book publisher branch that does not operate within the MLM as well), Monat, Scentsy, Pure Romance, Nerium, NuSkin, Origami Owl, ColorStreet, LipSense/Senegence, Advocare, Beauty Counter, Tastefully Simple, Thirty-One Bags, ItWorks!, Isagenix, Stella & Dot, Damsel in Defense, LegalShield, World Ventures, Cutco (and all other branches of Vector Marketing), Primerica, and of course, the scariest of them all, AMWAY. (Amway also has other branches, including Quixtar.)

Of course, if you're reading this book, I'm hoping that you're planning to start your *own* business!

But this Other Business Book I Read Said I Could Make it Big as an Avon Lady!

That other business book you read lied to you. Sorry. Like I've been saying throughout this book, identifying a target audience and target customer is necessary; and these #bossbabe-style business books (I won't name any names, so let's just call one of the worst culprits *Female Friend, Please Cease Expressing Remorse*), realize that their target demographic is women in their late twenties through early forties; they likely have kids, and are likely struggling with the pressures that both society and the economy place on working moms. They are the *same* target audience that MLMs go after. So, of course, these books will treat MLMs like a valid career choice; after all, a good percentage of their audience might already be in one.

So no, you're not going to make it big as an Avon lady. Maybe in 1980, you could have made a reasonable secondary income as an Avon lady. But as I mentioned before, in today's world of social media, joining an oversaturated, oversupplied, under-demanded market will do you no favors.

Don't be a #bossbabe and join an MLM. Be a #savvybusinessowner and start something new and creative!

4

How I Set Up My LLC

I was drunk on bourbon, sitting on a toilet in the back of a bar in Chicago, when it hit me: I really need to register an LLC. I came back from the bathroom, slid back into our booth at the bar, and announced to Tyler, "I'm going to register an LLC!"

The next morning, my hungover ass didn't even bother changing out of my pajamas before I walked to the bank to set up a business account. In the waiting room at the bank, I filled out IRS paperwork on my phone. A banker came into the waiting room and told me I'd have to wait two hours for an appointment. I said, "Sounds good," and went to the tattoo and piercing shop across the street from the bank. I got a new piercing in each ear. Then I went to Subway and ate a veggie sub full of

49

Actual helpful story

chipotle mayo. Then, I went back to the bank, gave them the new tax ID the IRS had sent me, and set up a business account.

The Furever Home Friends, LLC, was born.

And that's how I spent my first day of spring break during my first year of grad school.

Setting up my LLC was a lot easier than I expected. It required a bit of paperwork and a small fee to the state of Illinois (which was annoying), but nothing like what I'd been expecting.

To those who are new at business, some of these terms might not make sense, and some parts of this process might be a little confusing, so I will try to break down everything as best I can. This information should be helpful for authors as well; I have heard many of my author friends debating whether they should set up an LLC and what that process was like.

As a quick disclaimer: I have only ever set up an LLC in the state of Illinois. I know different states can sometimes have different processes and requirements, so I apologize if any of this information is different in your state. Also, if you are reading this from Canada, the UK, or any other country, this advice may not apply to you. My apologies. But like I said, this book is going to be me telling you guys what *I* did, so hopefully it's still helpful!

#SAVVYBUSINESSOWNER yes!,!

What is an LLC?

LLC stands for Limited Liability Company. Simply put, having an LLC separates *you* from *your business*. If your business is a separate entity from you as a person, you minimize the risk to your own personal life and assets. For example, if your LLC takes out a giant business loan and fails to pay it back, your business will go bankrupt and will probably die. But *you as a person* are protected from the government coming to take your house, car, or other assets away as a result.

In the United States, an LLC is not the only option for your business. You can also register as a sole proprietor, as a partnership, or as a corporation. Each of these options has its own laundry list of pros and cons, but in this chapter, we'll focus on the two forms I have experience with: an LLC and a sole proprietorship.

What is a Sole Proprietorship?

Before registering the Furever Home Friends as an LLC, I had registered a sole proprietorship in the past. In 2016, when I started offering freelance copyediting services to other writers, I decided to register myself as a sole proprietor for tax purposes. This was a full year before the Furever Home Friends even existed, so at the time, I was only

51

thinking of my "business" as myself: my YA novels, my editing services, etc. Things I created on my own.

If you're the only one involved in your business, registering yourself as a sole proprietor might be a good move. Basically, all being a sole proprietor means is that you're a one-person show.

Now, I'm not an accountant, so I'm not going to delve too deep into different tax benefits; it's not my area of expertise. However, I will say that registering as a sole proprietor makes sense if you want to avoid paying taxes as a company and instead pay only income taxes as an individual. The downside to a sole proprietorship is that the government doesn't recognize it as a "legal entity." It's not a "company"; it's just *you*. So, if you ever plan to expand your business with the help of investors or grants, you might have to change the way your business is registered.

As always, here's a big-ass disclaimer. If this were one of my YouTube videos, I'd have the word DISCLAIMER flashing across the screen in big red letters right now. Always talk to an accountant before choosing which way to register your business. Your accountant can give you the most accurate and up-to-date information regarding your state's laws.

Should You Start an LLC?

Honestly, if my own experience is anything to go by, I'd say yes, go ahead and register an LLC. (*Insert another annoying disclaimer here. Talk to an accountant first, consult with a lawyer, all of that.*) For me, the process was relatively easy. I just went onto Google and searched "register an LLC in Illinois." That led me to some forms I could fill out online. I also had to pay $250 to the state, which was annoying. However, if I'd tried to start a business a few years earlier, I would've had to pay $500 to the state, so at least it was better than that! Some have speculated that the Illinois government lowered the fees because too many people were heading out to Indiana or Iowa to start their businesses instead. I thought that was kind of funny. *lol's*

After you register your business with the state, you also have to register it with the IRS. For your taxes, you'll need to have an EIN, or Employer Identification Number. If your business is registered as a sole proprietorship instead of an LLC, you can use your own social security number as an EIN, and you don't need to register anything new with the IRS. But for an LLC, you need to get your business its own EIN.

Once I had my LLC registered and had received my EIN from the IRS, I was off to the bank to open a business bank account. If you remember the story I was telling at the beginning of the chapter, this process took all of 20 minutes, and I was in my pajamas for all of it. It was way less stressful than I had anticipated.

My appointment at the bank was also a lot less stressful—and way more *fun*—than I'd expected. But that could be because the bank near my apartment has a Keurig machine and these little caramel flavored coffee pods, and I can't resist those things to save my life. I met with a banker named Imran who had a cool beard. (I'm sure he still does, but I'm trying to keep my verb tenses consistent over here.) I told him all about the Furever Home Friends while he set up my account.

He was like, "That's so cool! Can I see one of the books?"

I pulled one of the books, *Princess Allee*, out of my bag. He was like, "My niece would love this. Can I buy it from you right now?"

And I was like, "Sure. Do you have a $10 bill?" And then I instantly felt like an idiot for asking that, because we were *currently at the bank*.

I left the bank that day with a debit card registered in the name of The Furever Home Friends, LLC. I got so excited that I just had to take a photo of it to send to all my friends and family and to post on social media. Of course, before I took the photo, I realized that taking a photo of your debit card number and sending it to people is THE

EASIEST WAY TO GET YOUR IDENTITY STOLEN. So, I covered up the number with my finger and just took a photo displaying the beautiful letters engraved in the plastic: FUREVER HOME FRIENDS.

Setting up my bank account was the only part of the process that I actually had to leave the house for. Maybe your bank lets you set up a new account over the phone or online, so call your bank to see what your options are.

However, the process of setting up the LLC itself was entirely online. I filed paperwork online through an Illinois government website and I obtained my EIN through irs.gov.

So, if you're planning to set up an LLC for your business, rest assured that, if your experience is anything like mine, it shouldn't be too stressful of a process. And if unexpected issues pop up, Google is your friend! And so am I! Like I said in the introduction, if you have any questions that you feel I didn't cover well enough in this chapter, feel free to email me at savyleiser@gmail.com and I'll give you the best information specific to YOUR business that I can.

Now, go on out there and become a registered business owner!

#SAVVYBUSINESSOWNER

PART 2

Starting with Startup Capital:

Do You Have to Spend Money to Make Money?

#SAVVYBUSINESSOWNER

5

What is Startup Capital?

We've all likely heard the expression, "You have to spend money to make money." Is that always true? No. You can make money in an infinite number of ways. But in this book, we're talking about starting your own business. So, yes, in the case of starting your own business, you *do* have to spend money to make money.

Now, if you're like I was when I started my business — under 25, still in school, not done paying off college loans, working a couple different jobs but not having any money left over to save — you might be wondering *where* you can get the money to start your business. Or, where you can get your *startup capital*.

Here, I'm using the phrase *startup capital* to refer to the money needed to get the basic pieces of your business up and running. That might be the first month's rent for a brick-and-mortar storefront. It might be the materials you need to create your products. It might be the manufacturing costs for your first minimum order. Basically, it's the money that you *need* for the business to have a snowball's chance in hell of even existing.

Some people just take a big chunk of money out of their own bank accounts and use that as their startup capital. If you have the money to do that, go for it. I won't stop you. However, these next few chapters will discuss the different ways to raise money to start your business, as well as my experiences with them. Each path has its own pros and cons, and I'll share what I learned while approaching each of them.

If you're like me, you might *also* have read a few business books that barely scratch the surface regarding how you can raise money to start your business. Many books assume you already have money, or your partner/spouse already has money, or your family already has money, or money doesn't matter. I don't understand why these books do that, especially when money is often the *biggest* barrier to entry for most people wanting to start their own business. It's not easy to start a graphic design business when you can't afford PhotoShop,

Truth :)

Illustrator, or a computer that can run design software. It's impossible to start a handmade crafting business if you can't afford the craft supplies. And it's ridiculously difficult to *grow* any type of established business if you don't have a budget for marketing, travel, advertisements, and more.

Some business books have suggested I hire a business coach, attend business development seminars, or join pay-to-play business networks or membership groups. These are all fine ideas on their own; in fact, a lot of these services can be extremely helpful to a new and emerging entrepreneur. But what these books have never told me is *how* these people paid for these events. I couldn't stand hearing, "I knew I couldn't afford it, but it was important to invest in myself, so I got the money and I went." Cool. Now, mind telling me *how* you got the money? Oh, that's never going to be addressed? Cool. In that case, I have no choice but to assume that you sold meth for a week. I do not recommend that. So instead, I'm going to walk you through the basics of raising startup capital.

There are three types of startup capital that I'm going to address in this book, each of which I'll explain in greater detail in the following chapters: crowdfunding, loans & credit, and venture capital.

Crowdfunding

This is likely going to be one of the longest chapters in the book. I have a *lot* of experience with crowdfunding. Kickstarter was how I raised the first $7,000 that I needed to hire illustrators, purchase ISBNs, and print the first run of books for The Furever Home Friends.

In short, crowdfunding is when you get small amounts of money from a large group of people, which all adds up into a decent-sized sum of money for *you*. Crowdfunding can be done through donations from people who want to see your business become a reality, or it can be done through pre-orders from people who want to buy your products before they release (or before you even have the money to create them).

Loans & Credit

I have combined my chapters on Loans & Credit and on Venture Capital. Both sections were *much* shorter than my crowdfunding section for one simple reason: I have a lot more experience with crowdfunding than I have with loans, credit, or venture capital.

Basically, loans and credit both involve borrowing money, usually from the bank. They are often difficult to secure and require interest on your payments. However, both loans and credit can be useful for many business owners, depending on the stage of their business and the size of the loan.

Venture Capital

Like I said, this book is going to be perfectly honest. I am not sacrificing honesty or full transparency in the name of making the book seem balanced or aesthetically pleasing. As a result, the section on Venture Capital will likely be one of the shortest sections in the book. Sorry if you're offended by books with chapters of wildly varying lengths.

The truth is, I have never used a venture capital investment. I want to present you with the option, because it exists, and I have basic knowledge of it. But I'm not going to pretend to go into detail about expertise I don't have.

With all of that in mind, let's talk about some of the different options for raising startup capital!

6

Crowdfunding: The Greatest Invention of the 21st Century!

So, you have a great idea for a product you want to sell someone. Maybe it's a photography collection that you can't afford to get printed in bulk. Maybe it's a new clothing line that you can't afford minimum quantity production for. Maybe it's a new app, invention, or piece of technology that you know how to create, but still need materials that you can't afford. Or maybe it's a book and toy series, just like it was for me back in 2017. You know that people want this item, and you know that you have the capability to create it once you have all the necessary materials; the only problem is that you can't afford to pay for those initial materials in the first place.

In 2017, I had *many* costs associated with starting the Furever Home Friends and I could afford approximately zero of them. Those expenses included getting the first run of my books printed, purchasing ISBN numbers from Bowker to generate barcodes for the books, and getting the initial materials to make the first set of stuffed animals. I also wanted each book to be illustrated by a different artist (I illustrated book three). I thought that a variety of different art styles would represent the beautiful diversity we often find among rescue dogs. Consequently, I had to pay two illustrators as well. I knew that people would want to buy these products once they existed. The question in my mind was, *how could I obtain the funds for the necessary materials to make these products exist in the first place?* The answer: preorders.

For a lot of newer businesses, crowdfunding can be used as a platform for taking preorders. Through those preorders, business owners raise the initial funds that they need to bring their business to life and, once they've received the money from their supporters, they can create and send out the products ordered.

With crowdfunding, preorders happen through a system called *reward tiers*. Regardless of platform, when you set up your reward tiers, you can set amounts that people can pledge to receive certain products. For example, since I sell my stuffed animals for $25, I would create a $25 reward tier for my Kickstarter campaign, which explained that everyone who pledged $25 would receive one stuffed animal as a reward. I also created a $50 reward tier for those who wanted *two* stuffed animals and a $100 reward tier for those who wanted all four. During my first campaign, I even went as low as having a $1 reward tier. The reward for $1 was that I would put your name on the "Acknowledgments" page in the back of the first two books as a thank-you. During my first campaign, I received pledges and preorders of my books, stuffed animals, or combinations from about 140 people, totaling just over $7,200.

Thank goodness for crowdfunding. Honestly, I think crowdfunding is one of the best inventions of the 21st century. There is so much opportunity to bring an idea to life through connecting directly with the people most interested.

In this chapter, I'm going to break down three crowdfunding platforms: Kickstarter, IndieGogo/GoFundMe, and Patreon. I'm also going to share my tips and best practices for crowdfunding at the end; raising thousands of dollars online is *not easy*. But it is *absolutely* doable!

Kickstarter is the platform I have used twice during my time running the Furever Home Friends. In sum, I have raised over $10,000 on Kickstarter from my two campaigns. In 2017, I ran my first Kickstarter campaign, which raised $7,200 to cover the costs of hiring two illustrators, ordering the first 200 copies of the books, and buying ISBNs. In 2019, I ran my second Kickstarter, which raised $3,600 to get the first 200 of each stuffed animal produced by a manufacturer.

What leaves many people fearful of Kickstarter is that it's an "all or nothing" platform. That means you set a funding goal and a deadline for yourself, and if you don't reach that amount of funding by your deadline, you get none of the money. No one's cards get charged, and Kickstarter doesn't take anything either. Financially, it's as if the campaign never existed.

Why would anyone want to do that? Trust me, that's what I first thought when I was learning about Kickstarter and considering it for my business. Why not use a different funding site that allows you to keep the money even if you fall short of the goal? However, after thinking it over and considering what my actual *goal* was with crowdfunding—to use it as a platform for taking preorders—it made a lot more sense to take the all-or-nothing approach.

Think of it this way. Imagine you need $10,000 to buy the minimum quantity of T-shirts and jackets for your new clothing business. People start pledging for your clothes and selecting which items they want as rewards for their payment. Now, let's say that at the end of your campaign, you receive only $8,000 in funding. That's great, right? You'd rather *have* that money than *not* have it, right? Well, not really. If you receive that $8,000, that means that everyone who preordered a T-shirt or a jacket just got their credit card charged for that purchase. But you needed *all* of the $10,000 for the *minimum* order—you are unable to produce the clothes until you have $2,000 more, and you're now stuck with hundreds of angry customers waiting on products that you can't deliver.

I was in a similar place. If I didn't have enough money to pay the illustrators, the books *couldn't* get produced. If I didn't have the money in my bank account to pay the manufacturer for the minimum-order run of stuffed animals, I *couldn't* get *any* produced. I needed to figure out the minimum amount of money that I *needed* to make *any* orders possible.

What that required was a ton of math! I needed to figure out what the absolute *minimum* I needed for my Kickstarter campaign was. It would suck to set my goal at $10,000, fall short by a thousand or so, and then later realize that I could have produced everything for $8,000. It would also suck to set my goal for $3,000 and then realize that I couldn't even start production for less than $7,000.

So, before starting my campaign, I took a few things into account. First, how much did I have in my personal bank account that I could use as a last resort? Second, how much would I have to pay for basics to get the books completed? For illustrations and ISBNs for my first two books, I realized I would need about $4,500. To reach that $4,500 in pledges, if I sold books at $15 apiece, how many books would I need to sell? Once I had that number, I had to calculate how much it would cost to get all of those books printed. After a *lot* of calculations, I found that the *minimum* I could get by on was $7,000; as a result, my first Kickstarter campaign had a $7,000 goal.

There were times during that first campaign when funding was slow, and I'd wonder, *Man, why didn't I just make my goal $3,000? Then I'd be guaranteed the money!* or, *Why didn't I choose IndieGoGo or another platform that would let me keep the money regardless of whether I met the goal?* But then, I'd remember that without $7,000, I would have *no way* to produce the books and the first run of plushies. I would be stuck with customers who ordered something, and I'd be scrambling to find other ways to quickly get cash to pay for the rest of production. That would be a terrible situation to be in, especially when trying to start a new business and gain the trust of brand-new customers.

After two successful Kickstarter campaigns, I can confidently say that I'm glad I used that platform. However, that doesn't mean Kickstarter is the right platform for *everybody*. Other sites, like IndieGogo and Patreon, might be an even better way to achieve your startup capital goals.

IndieGogo and GoFundMe

What do IndieGogo and GoFundMe have in common? Unlike Kickstarter, they do *not* require you to reach your full funding goal to receive any of the money (though IndieGogo lets you choose an all-or-nothing option if you want). If you're in a position where receiving full funding isn't a necessity, these platforms may be a better choice, since Kickstarter can get *stressful* when you're nearing the end of the campaign!

For example, let's say you own a small handmade jewelry business. You can currently buy materials in small quantities and have enough materials in stock to produce your main pieces. However, you'd really like to put together an advertising budget and save up for the first month of rent at a brick-and-mortar store.

In this case, you could try a site like IndieGogo or GoFundMe. You can offer your jewelry — which you already have the supplies and means to make — as rewards, but set a funding goal consistent with your future plans. Even if you don't make the full goal, you will still be able to fulfill your customers' orders and you will have made some progress toward your expansion goal.

I've seen IndieGogo and GoFundMe used for film and music production projects as well. Often, aspiring filmmakers or music producers have the bare minimum they need — a camera, a microphone, some basic recording and editing equipment — to get started, but would like to upgrade for a new project. Using a site like IndieGogo or GoFundMe helps them raise some money for a higher budget; however, if they don't make *everything* they need for that particular camera model, they can still produce the project and give it to backers, and can structure their upgrades according to the amount of money earned.

Patreon

If your business idea involves producing some form of recurring content, then a site like Patreon may be for you. I have a small amount of experience with Patreon — I have a page with a handful of supporters (shoutout to all of you over on the acknowledgments page!). Patreon can be useful to people trying to start a business that involves recurring productions or that creates digital products, such as videos or podcasts.

With Patreon, fans and supporters can sign up as "patrons," which basically means they pay you a monthly subscription; that's why Patreon is best for those creating something on a recurring basis, such as music, videos, art/comics, short stories, or podcast episodes.

For example, let's say you want to start up a business as an indie rapper. You could set up a Patreon page where everyone who pays $1 a month receives frequent behind-the-scenes photos and updates about your recording process. Everyone who pays $5 a month gets access to all the new songs you produced that month. If you're producing physical CDs or merch, maybe people who pledge even higher can get those things as well.

However, if you are looking to just raise a bunch of money at once to start production for your business, Patreon may not be for you. People who pledge money on Patreon are often looking for frequently recurring content, such as new weekly podcast episodes, comic strips that regularly update, or daily YouTube video uploads.

Just like we've discussed in this book, each of these platforms has its own *target audience* and its own features that make it appealing to people with different business goals. Regardless of the platform you choose, however, there are some best practices for crowdfunding that you should keep in mind as you plan your first campaign.

My Best Tips for Crowdfunding

Raising over 10 grand through crowdfunding was *not easy*. It came with a buttload of challenges that I didn't expect when I first made my page. However, after two successful campaigns, I have learned *so much* about what makes a campaign successful. The short answer? A *lot of work*. The long answer? A *llloooottttt of wwwooorrrrkkkk.*

In all seriousness, though, here are my best tips for running a successful crowdfunding campaign:

Tell Your Story!

Have you ever browsed Kickstarter for new products you might be interested in preordering, only to find a page that looks like it was written by a robot? The product's features are laid out before you in technical, factual terms. Maybe their video was even recorded by text-to-speech software instead of a human. Often, these projects are *really* far away from their funding goal. And I usually click right off of them.

New customers need something they can connect to on a personal and emotional level. If this new product sounds like it was produced by a faceless corporation, then your customers will feel like they'd be better off just buying an inexpensive, comparable version of it at Target. People who pledge to crowdfunding campaigns want to connect with the *person* who's starting this business; they want to know that the person creating their new favorite brand is someone they can trust.

Start by telling your story. In your project description on your page, talk about who *you* are: what makes you qualified to start this business? Why do you feel so passionately about it? Where did you first get the idea for it?

For example, let's say that you want to start up a business that makes clothes out of recycled materials. There's got to be a story behind that, right? Maybe you got the idea from watching a documentary about how the fast fashion industry is hurting the environment over time. Maybe designing clothes has been your lifelong passion. Tell *that* story when you're starting your page.

However, telling your story goes beyond just writing it out in the project's description. You also need to...

Make an Awesome Video!

Most people enjoy some kind of visual stimulation. Just look at the popularity of TV shows, movies, and video games! A video on your page is a great way to catch people's attention, help them get to know you and your story on a deeper level, and show them physical examples of your products.

Your video should be no longer than three or four minutes long. You want to make sure you're capturing your audience's attention and concisely giving them all of the information they need to make a purchasing decision. You don't want to lose their attention for a second, which, on the internet, is *not easy*. When planning out your crowdfunding video, take a piece of advice from former President Franklin D. Roosevelt: "Be sincere; be brief; be seated."

So, what *should* your video include? First, keep in mind that film is a *visual* medium. It sounds obvious, but I can't tell you how many Kickstarter videos I've seen where the person is just talking to their phone like they're on an Instagram story. I'm sure your face is beautiful, but probably not enough to make me pull out my credit card—unless the business you're planning to start is in a *very* different industry.

I like to start off my videos with a quick montage that captures what the Furever Home

Friends is all about. This might be two seconds of Chewie being cute, followed by three seconds or so of the plushies bopping around to some music, followed by a sped-up shot of me flipping through the books' pages. Within a few seconds, you know that the business is about dogs, plushies, and books. From there, I usually start talking directly to the audience about my business.

This is where you *do* want to show your face. Make sure that you're not just recording a voiceover; show yourself to the camera! Just make sure you're filming it in landscape orientation. A video shot vertically on a phone looks casual, like it belongs on your personal social media.

In your video, make sure to include a brief history of the business, why it matters to you, why you need to use crowdfunding to raise money, and most importantly, *what exactly* the pledge money will be going toward. *Why* do you need the money? Are you going to spend 50% of your goal amount on minimum product orders, 20% on advertising, and 30% on obtaining licensure? Then, make sure to give an overview of the rewards available if someone pledges.

But Savy… you said I have to keep my video to three minutes! How can I do all of that in such a short video? My recommendation is to write out a script ahead of time for what you'll say in your video. Then, take out a stopwatch or your phone timer and

Great advice!

practice reading it. See how long it's taking. Then, start editing it down to *just the bare minimum*. When I was in grad school, my journalism professor once told me that writing a magazine article was about "putting every word on trial for its life." When you're trying to share a *ton* of information in a short amount of time, make sure each word in your script *counts*.

To make a crowdfunding video, you don't need expensive high-end equipment. I mean, that would be crazy, right? You'd have to start a whole second campaign just to raise the money to buy a camera and microphone! Don't worry about any of that; you can make an informative and professional video on a small budget.

If your phone's camera takes high-quality pictures and videos, go ahead and use that! Many phones don't capture clear audio, however. For both of my Kickstarter videos, I used a Snowball microphone that I purchased on Amazon for about $40. There are also less expensive microphone options available as well. Or, if your phone *does* take clear audio, then you're one of the lucky ones! Just be sure to test it ahead of time.

Once you've shot your video, it's time for editing! Some editing programs can be expensive, and some can be difficult to navigate. I still get flashbacks to my time trying to work AVID while working on student films in college. But you don't need to use Hollywood-caliber editing tools to make your video awesome. If you already have the Adobe Creative Suite, I highly recommend using Premiere for editing videos. It isn't difficult to learn. If you can't pay for Adobe software (I couldn't either), there are lots of free options available. If you have an Apple computer, it should come with iMovie already installed. If you don't have a Mac — or if you don't like iMovie (which I find very limiting in its capabilities and annoying to use) — then you can download Lightworks for free. Lightworks is what I use to edit all my YouTube videos; so, if you enjoy my channel, maybe give Lightworks a try!

Make Your Page Financially Transparent

Remember how, in the video section, I mentioned that you should break down *exactly* what all the money will be used for? This should also be in your project description. The more specific and transparent you can be about the financial breakdown of your project, the more trust you will inspire in potential backers.

I have seen *way* too many crowdfunding projects that are vague and shady with their funding goals. I have *never* backed a project that says, "We need $50,000 to make this movie!" if it can't break down how much is going to equipment rentals, location permits, actor stipends, etc. Most pages I've seen will say something like, "We need $50,000 to make this movie!" and then nothing more.

Your potential customers want to know *how* their money will help you. If they pledge ten dollars to preorder a T-shirt, will those ten dollars bring you one percent closer to being able to put in a minimum order with a manufacturer? *Tell them.*

On my first Kickstarter page, I broke down how much money was going to pay for illustrations (about $4,500), how much was going to book printing (about $1,000), how much was going to stuffed animal materials for our first run (again, about $1,000), and how much was set aside as a buffer for taxes (about $500). The more open you can be about where your funds are going, the more your potential customers will trust you.

The First Week: A Social Media Launch

When's the last time you bought something the *first* time you saw an ad for it? Especially on the *internet*? On social media, we're bombarded with ads everywhere we look, from sponsored ads on Facebook, to other small business owners in our feed posting about their own products, to the ads playing before YouTube videos. Chances are, if you've seen an ad *one time* online, you're not instantly going to buy.

The same idea goes for crowdfunding. If you post on your social media on launch day, very few people are going to pledge from that alone. Most people who see it might think, "Oh, that looks cool. Maybe I'll pledge to that campaign or preorder that product later." And then they forget about it. A thousand other images are bombarding them online, and their attention has snapped to something else.

Instead, develop a social media strategy. For your first week, plan out a series of posts on all platforms you use—I recommend posting on Facebook, Twitter, and Instagram at minimum—and schedule one post per day on each site. Make each post different; create different graphic featuring your products (I recommend the website Canva for free, easy graphic design), add captions that discuss the products from different angles, and always, *always* include a direct link to your crowdfunding page. Within the first week, your followers should have seen the posts a couple of times.

One thing to keep in mind, though, is that social media algorithms are constantly changing. When I ran my second Kickstarter (a 30-day campaign running from May to June of 2019), Facebook's algorithm had just begun de-prioritizing posts from Kickstarter. The reason was that Facebook was launching their own crowdfunding platform and saw Kickstarter as competition. Yes, the Zuck is *that* petty.

Because algorithms are constantly changing and are unpredictable, that's even more reason to post *often*. While I can't predict how the social media algorithms will react during your crowdfunding campaign, I will say that in my experience, most social media sites react well to *consistency*. The more often you post, the more likely your post is to be seen.

When it comes to my social media strategy during a crowdfunding campaign, I like to plan out my posts ahead of time. We business owners all must strike that balance on our social media between interaction and self-promotion. No one wants to follow someone on Instagram who just posts a graphic full of text saying "CONTRIBUTE TO MY KICKSTARTER" every day.

When I'm running a crowdfunding campaign, I plan to post to all my social media platforms every day, but for my promotional posts to be the MINIMUM of my content. What that means is that I'm posting at least 3-4 times a day on each platform, with one post being about the campaign and all the others being about other things: pictures of Chewie, video game screenshots, photos of my writing process, pictures of pretty mugs I have in my kitchen, etc.

During the last week of my Kickstarters, I've usually posted daily countdowns on my social media. Before my campaign even starts, I'll make graphics for Instagram (often on Canva or a similar site) with a cute picture of my books & plushies and text that says, "1 week to go!" "6 days to go!" "5 days to go!" and so on until I reach "LAST DAY!"

The reason the countdowns are important is that they not only remind people that the campaign is there, but that time is running out. Scarcity drives customers to take action. (However, I'd never condone *faking* scarcity; some sites have done that by falsely advertising how much time or stock is left. That's shady and dishonest, and it's important to build a trustworthy relationship with your customers.) In the case of a Kickstarter, there IS a scarcity of time. If you don't reach your funding goal before the deadline, you won't get the funds! There's nothing wrong with reminding your customers of that.

Email Newsletter Updates

Social media is constantly changing. Every time we turn around, it feels like there's been another Thanos snap. As I'm writing this, Tumblr has recently dug its own grave by censoring all of its porn artists, who arguably made up a decent percentage of their user base. Basically, social media is unpredictable. It's *necessary*, but it's unpredictable.

If only there could be something stable and long-lasting on the internet! Luckily… we still have email. A lot of business owners make the mistake of thinking email is dead, instead prioritizing the hottest new social media platform. The truth is, you need both email *and* social media. But email has an advantage; it's *yours*. Lately, we've seen controversial political figures get "de-platformed," or removed from social media sites like Twitter and Facebook. Regardless of political leanings, we can all learn from this; social media is unreliable. However, your list of email contacts is *yours*. Your email address is *yours*.

Before beginning your first crowdfunding campaign, try to gather a list of email contacts. You can do this through going to networking events with a clipboard and asking others if they'd like to join. If you already have a thriving business, you can have an email list sign-up box on your website or take a physical sign-up sheet to events. During your crowdfunding campaign, send out three emails: one during the launch, one at the halfway point, and one right before the end during your final push.

But Savy! You said that crowdfunding was a way to start a business from nothing. What if I don't have an email list? Well, then start small. Start by emailing friends, family, and other people you know. Just keep one thing in mind: if someone ever asks to be removed from your email list, you *always* remove them, no questions asked. Oh, and you *never* sell your email list to another company. *Ever.*

Tell EVERYONE You Know!

The above heading may seem obvious. Tell everyone you know? *Savy, isn't that what you just explained to me? To email everyone I know and post about it on social media, where everyone I know will see it?* Nope. Here, I'm talking about telling everyone you know *individually*. Nothing beats good old-fashioned one-on-one communication.

In April 2017, I was halfway through my first Kickstarter campaign—in terms of days elapsed, that is. *Not* in terms of money raised. I had less than half of my campaign—less than two weeks, actually—to go, and I hadn't even hit the $2,000 mark yet. Since I needed to raise $7,000, it wasn't looking good.

I looked at some of the successful Kickstarters in my category (books) and found their creators on Twitter. I sent out some DMs to those other authors to get some advice. *What did they do to raise so much money that I'm overlooking*, I wondered.

The response? *Message everyone you know individually and tell them about it.* My immediate reaction to that? *No. F-ing. Way.* In my head, messaging *everyone you know*, including people you haven't seen since high school, is what MLM and pyramid scheme participants do! It's what everyone thinks is annoying and scammy and awful! But the more I thought about it, the more I realized that maybe it didn't *have* to be awful and scammy — if I approached it the right way.

That night, I sent out three messages. I was nervous the entire time; my friends were going to hate me! They were going to say, "Ew, Savy, I thought you were cool, but now you're advertising to me?" They were going to block me and cancel me and my social life would be over! After sending those three messages, I put my phone on silent and turned it face-down so I couldn't see the replies. I was so scared.

I came back a few hours later, only to find that my project had $100 more added, and I had a few messages waiting for me. They said things like, "Actually, I hadn't seen your posts about this! This is so cool! I'll share it with my friends!" and, "I meant to order one of these plushies but forgot about it! Thanks for the reminder! Ordering now!"

<u>Dos and Don'ts for Reaching Out to Every Single Person You Know</u>

 DO include their name in the message. Greet them!

DON'T start the message with, "Hey girl!" or "Hey bro!" or, worst of all, "Hey hun!"

 DO make it clear why you're reaching out to them. For example, I'll say something like, "I'm not sure if you saw my posts on social media, but our campaign has only 3 days left to succeed. If we don't reach our goal, we get none of the money."

 DON'T judge someone based on whether they order from you. You're starting a handmade jewelry company, and your best friend of all time doesn't buy any? Well, maybe they don't wear jewelry. Maybe they're tight on money at the moment. Maybe they just think your jewelry is ugly and don't like it. It has literally zero impact on your friendship. Get over it and talk to them about something else.

 DO offer options for support other than buying. For example, I like to say things like, "If you're interested in preordering, that would be amazing! But if you're unable to buy anything, that's totally fine too! I would really appreciate it if you could either share the link on your social media or tell anyone you know who might be interested."

 DON'T reach out more than once. EVER. If you reach out to 1,000 people, chances are, a few hundred won't even reply to your message. Do not follow up. Do not say, "Hey, I don't know if you saw my message the other day, but…" Do not pass go. Do not collect $200 (from this person, anyway; they're obviously not interested in buying). Instead, I recommend just talking to that person about something completely different and never bringing it up again. *But Savy, how will that help my crowdfunding campaign?* It won't. But it will help you remember that your friends, family, and followers are more than just customers, and it will give you the opportunity to catch up with an old friend.

DO continue the conversation outside of the sales pitch. If someone replies to you with a non-committal message like, "Oh, that sounds cool!", then respond with, "How has your new job been?" or "How's your dog doing?" or something that shows you genuinely care about them as a person. If you *don't* actually care about them as a person, don't reach out to them; that's just weird. I guess what I'm getting at is, if you don't actually *want* to have a conversation with every person you've ever met in your life *right now*, then don't even reach out to anyone. You need to be genuine.

Update Regularly!

One of the reasons people love contributing to crowdfunding campaigns is that they can get a "behind the scenes" look at the process behind creating a product. That's why it's fun for them to preorder from your crowdfunding page rather than wait for the product to hit shelves. To keep these customers involved in the process, you'll want to post regular updates to your page.

So, how do updates work? On Kickstarter, updates work kind of like a blog post. You can add new posts to your campaign, and all your backers will be notified via email that a new update has been posted. This will keep them invested in the process.

What goes into an update? Well, I like to think of updates as four parts: an expression of gratitude, a look behind the scenes of the production process, an update on your business's progress, and a call to action.

That might look something like this:

Expression of Gratitude: Hey, friends! It's time for another Furever Home Friends PUPdate! Thank you all so much for your preorders or contributions to this campaign! I'm so happy that you support this business's mission.

<u>Behind the Scenes:</u> Today, I had a phone call with the stuffed animal manufacturer, and the final designs have been approved! See the picture below for what the final designs look like!

<u>Update:</u> We're getting really close to our final goal of $3,500. Right now, we're over 75% of the way there with two weeks to go — that's amazing! Again, thank you so much for your help.

<u>Call to Action:</u> It would mean the world to me if you could share this campaign with any friends, family, or dog lovers in your life who might be interested. Feel free to tag @fureverhomefriends on Instagram if you share any pictures!

Then, I'll usually have a sign-off that says something like "Love, Savy & Chewie." (Chewie is my business partner. He's also the official receptionist of Furever Home Friends Headquarters, which currently takes up two rooms of my apartment. Yay, mortgage tax write-offs!)

So, how often should you update? Well, the easy answer is that you should update whenever something significant happens. For example, during my stuffed animal campaign, I updated when I received the mock-up photos from the manufacturer, when I received the prototypes of the four plushies in the mail, etc. During my book campaign, I updated when artists sent me the outlines for their illustrations, when I got my first full-color pictures, when the cover design was complete, etc. Generally, if you can take a picture of something to show your audience, that is a great time to update!

The more difficult answer is that you need to balance the frequency of your updates. Updating every single day will inundate your backers with email notifications, meaning many of them are going straight to the trash can. Think about it: how often do you see five emails a day from a company or a product you like and just instantly delete them without thinking? For me, it's fairly often. However, if that company is sending me an interesting update every week, I'm more likely to at least open the email. I tried to update once or twice a week during both of my campaigns.

I won't lie: crowdfunding isn't easy, and it definitely has a learning curve. In the many articles I read about crowdfunding before I launched my first campaign, and in the many Facebook groups I joined to talk about Kickstarter, I frequently saw people saying that running a crowdfunding campaign felt like having a second full-time job. People were spending 4-8 hours a day just promoting their campaigns during its 30-day run. That was my experience as well. During my campaigns, I blocked out four hours every evening to focus on telling people about the campaign, reaching out to bloggers and social media personalities, etc.

Crowdfunding can be straight-up *exhausting*. But in the long run, I found it incredibly beneficial for getting my business off the ground. And the truth is, there aren't many ways to raise startup capital that *aren't* exhausting. Making money is exhausting by nature. But hey, so is running a business. Get ready to be tired with me!

7

The Pros & Cons of Loans, Credit & Venture Capital

Growing Pains is more than just one of the cheesiest sitcoms to ever come out of the 80s. It's also a regular part of every business's expansion process. As entrepreneurs, we'll often hit a point where we think, *Damn, if only I had $10 grand more, I could completely turn this business around*! As the term "growing pains" would suggest, growing a business can be *painful*, and not just to your overworked, exhausted body; your wallet is probably going to hurt most of all.

A lot of businesses will alleviate this pain with the sweet, sweet balm of borrowed money. Getting a business loan, line of credit, or credit card might be a great decision for you, or it might not be. The same thing goes for pursuing an investment. In this chapter, I intend to break down some of the pros and cons of loans, credit, and investments.

As a disclaimer, keep in mind that this chapter is just intended to give you background information on these options and to share my personal experience with them. Always remember to talk these decisions through with bankers, lawyers, accountants, and a bunch of other people who make way more money than I do.

In mid-2019, I realized it was time for me to get serious about scaling the Furever Home Friends to the next level. I had just graduated from DePaul University with my Master's, and I was ready to devote full-time hours to this business. Of course, those were full-time hours *on top of* my two part-time jobs: teaching creative writing classes to kids and writing articles for music magazines. But by no longer going to school, my workweeks drastically reduced, dropping from about 95 hours of working per week to 60 hours a week. Chewie was so, so happy to see his human home with him more often! So was Tyler.

I recognized that the next step in scaling my business would require *money*. I wanted to start pursuing retail stores, selling my products at larger events, and increasing my profit margins overall.

Because I was getting my books printed in small quantities, I was paying over $3 *per book* in printing costs. Since the books have full-color interiors, that may not sound like a lot. But I like to sell paperbacks for $10. (If you're reading this book in like 2050 or something, and inflation has made books cost way more, then just scale it all down.) After paying to get the books printed and shipped to me in small quantities, the per-book cost ended up being around $4.25.

When selling to stores, I obviously needed to sell the books at a discount so the store could make a profit as well. With most stores, I do a 40% discount. So, if I was selling each book for $10 on my website and at events, that meant brick-and-mortar stores could buy the books from me for $6. Well, if the store is paying $6, and I'm paying $4.25 to print and ship each book, what does that leave me with? That's right: $1.75 profit per book. The traditional publishing industry has conditioned authors to think that's a good royalty. And yeah, it might be. But I'm not working for royalties. As a business owner, I could see that my profit margins were *abysmal*.

I'd gotten the suggestion to raise my book prices. Surely selling a paperback for $12 instead of $10 wouldn't make a huge difference, right? And while that might be true, I've found that $10 is the sweet spot for my books. Because I frequently sell at events, festivals, conventions, and fairs, having a round price like $10 makes it easy for customers to just whip a $10 bill out of their wallet, or to hand me a $20 if they want two books. Plus, I've received enough compliments about how much people like my pricing to recognize a good thing when it's in front of me.

After talking with another author friend of mine, who also runs his own business, the solution was obvious: I needed to decrease my production costs. This author was getting full-color *hardcovers* printed for $2 per book because he was buying them in bulk quantities from overseas. He recommended a printing company in Hong Kong to me, and I contacted them for a quote. Soon, I found that I could get my paperbacks printed and shipped to me for about $1 apiece — *if* I bought 4,000 of them.

Now, I don't know about you, but I don't just have $4,000 lying around. (If you do, that's awesome, and I'm jealous as hell.) Plus, keep in mind that most businesses take a loss over their first five years of operation, mine included. Everything I was making was going back into the business for expansion costs: advertisements, product orders, development of new products, etc.

Now Savy, you might be asking, *what about your childhood stock-trading phase you mentioned in Chapter 1? Couldn't you just take that surprise stock-market money and use that for the bulk printing costs?*

No, because I'd already spent almost all of that money (along with the money raised during my second Kickstarter) to get 600 stuffed animals produced. Writing this section right now is hard, because I'm worried that you, the reader, are going to look at me and think, *Wow, Savy was really hurting for money. What a loser. Why would I ever take Savy's business advice now?* And you don't have to if you don't want to. But I think it's important to be honest about our journeys as entrepreneurs. A lot of the process *is* having no money. I did not become wealthy overnight. In fact, I'm not even wealthy *now*. But like I said in the introduction, this book isn't to teach you how to get rich. It's to share my experience and advice for bringing your business vision to life.

So, when I had nowhere near the $4,000 (plus tariffs) I'd need to get the books bulk printed, I thought about doing what many business owners have found success with: getting a business loan.

What are Loans? What is Credit?

I met with Imran, the same cool bearded banker I talked about in Chapter 4. We went over the process of applying for a business loan, for a line of credit, and for a credit card. In the end, I decided not to move forward with these options, and I'll explain why. However, these options might be great for you, so I'll break down what I've learned here.

I'm sure everyone reading this already has a basic understanding of what a loan is; actually, if I know my core audience, most of you are probably in the process of paying off loans from college (I still am, too). You probably also have some experience with credit from using a credit card. And you probably know the worst part of both loans and credit: *interest*.

Pros of Loans & Credit

During my meeting at the bank, I discussed my options for borrowing money, which included a business loan, a line of credit, and a credit card. The main selling point of a loan is that you can generally take out more money with a lower interest rate. Many business loans start at about $25,000. However, it was difficult for me to get approved for a business loan because my company was still so small and didn't have enough revenue within the past year to build trust with the bank.

My second loan option was a home equity loan. Because Tyler and I own our apartment, we could borrow money equivalent to the increase in the property's value since we bought it. The main pro of this type of loan is that, as a homeowning couple who had never been late on a mortgage payment, we were likely to get approved for it.

Now, I was only looking to borrow $5-10,000, which is why I also discussed a line of credit and a credit card. A major selling point for taking out credit instead of a loan is that it's easier to get approved for credit without the bank looking into all your financial files from the past few years.

Learning about each of these options left me with a lot to consider, especially since each one came with its own set of downsides as well.

Cons of Loans & Credit

The main downside of a business loan, for me, was that I was unlikely to get approved for it. Plus, it would be stressful to have borrowed *that much money*—$25,000 is more than I owe for college loans—and be on the hook to pay all of it back.

I barely even considered the home equity loan. Remember in Chapter 4, when I talked about how one of the major benefits of having an LLC is that, in the case of business failure, you're protected from the government taking your home away? Yeah, a home equity loan would completely screw *all of that* up.

To take out a home equity loan, Tyler and I would have to apply for it as a human couple, not as a business. That was frightening to us. Now, maybe to you, that doesn't sound scary; in that case, go for it. But Tyler and I decided as a couple that I would keep my business separate from our personal expenses. Risking *other people's* money when starting a business is terrifying to me, even if it's a spouse whom I share personal finances with. So, while we were likely to get approved for a large home equity loan, I was unwilling to risk our home for my business, especially when there were other options available.

One of those other options was to get a business credit card. The credit card available to me had a $10,000 limit, which would more than cover the costs I needed to get my books printed in bulk. It also had no interest — for the first 9 months.

I did consider this option. I figured, if my plan is to start selling the books to brick-and-mortar stores, plus make money at larger events, the increased profit margin would make it easy to pay back all the money I'd spent on the credit card.

But, that voice in my head said, what if something outside your control happens and you *can't* pay off the card in the first 9 months? Then you'll be stuck with interest — which, in the case of this business credit card, was about 24 percent. So, if I spent $5,000 to get 4,000 books printed and shipped, I wouldn't just have to pay back $5,000, I'd have to pay back $6,200! And if I had to space out those payments even longer over time, the interest would keep building up, and who *knows* how expensive that might be? At that point, I'd be better off sticking to small-quantity printing and taking the lower profit margin!

At the time (early 2019) I felt pretty confident that I could make back $5,000 and *more* pretty quickly and would never have to pay that interest. But that nagging little voice in my head kept saying, "What if you don't? What if you *can't*?"

I'm so glad I listened to that voice and didn't get the credit card. If you're reading this book right now, that means it's late 2020 at the earliest. We all know what happened in 2020: the coronavirus pandemic.

No one could have predicted that a virus would take over pretty much the entire world and cause almost everything to be shut down. All of my events from mid-March 2020 on were canceled for the year. No more BookCon. No more pet expos. No more craft fairs or small business expos. And NO brick-and-mortar stores. Most of my opportunities to make money selling a large quantity of books disappeared instantly. Thank goodness I'm not stuck with accruing interest or an angry bank.

This section isn't to say that you *shouldn't* get a credit card, loan, or line of credit if that works for you. If you thoroughly weigh the pros and cons, make a timeline for yourself to pay it back, and find yourself confident that you can make it work, then go for it! But I'd just recommend exercising caution. While I'm typing this sentence, it's the end of May 2020, and we're currently over 75 days into quarantine. The pandemic of 2020 has wreaked havoc on the small business community, and I'm grateful not to owe money to a bank right now.

What is Venture Capital?

Have you ever watched *Shark Tank*, pretending that it made you above all the other reality-TV addicts out there because *your show* was about *business*? If the answer is yes, then I have some news for you: you're not any better than anyone else who enjoys reality TV. But on the bright side, there's nothing wrong with enjoying reality TV, and I'm a *huge* fan of *Shark Tank* as well.

Shows like *Shark Tank* provide one of the most accessible looks into the world of venture capital.

Venture capital, at its most basic definition, is a fancy way of saying "investors." If a group of venture capitalists take interest in your business, they might give you a large sum of money up front in exchange for a share of equity in the business. Basically, it's like you're selling stock in your business. If the value of your business increases, that will pay off for your investors. If you ever sell your business to a larger company, your investors will get whatever percentage of your earnings that they own.

Now, I don't have a ton to say about venture capital, as it's not a route I've yet tried for my business. But let's go over some brief pros and cons anyway!

Pros of Venture Capital

It's not a loan. You don't owe anyone money. That's the biggest advantage, in my opinion. If your business fails, you aren't stuck with a big bank breathing down your neck asking where the money is.

Also, venture capitalists are often looking to make large investments. In the case of a small business, that's both a pro and a con, depending on the situation. It might be hard to find an investor if your business is new, has a small customer base, and is bringing in less than $50,000 a year in revenue. That's the case with Furever Home Friends — we are *small*.

Cons of Venture Capital

Someone might try to buy you out. Since I mentioned in the Pros section that many venture capitalists are looking for large-scale investments, if you have a small business, an investor might only see it as worth their time if they buy the entire company. Notice I said *might* — feel free to still look for an investor, since this isn't a guarantee.

Along with an investor putting money in your business, they gain at least some level of ownership. Even if you sell only 15 percent or 10 percent of your company, you are no longer the sole owner. The more investors you get, the less in charge YOU are of major decisions, such as the possibility of selling your company in the future. If an investor offers to buy over 50 percent of the business, you might lose control of the ability to make key decisions about your own company.

How Can I Decide?

As you know, after I weighed all the pros and cons of loans, credit, and venture capital, my choice was: none of them. If you read the previous chapter, you know that my choice for startup capital was crowdfunding, as I've found that to be the best way to earn money, grow a customer base, and retain full control of my company and my finances. But that might not be the right course of action for you!

When making a decision about what avenue to pursue, especially financially, it's important to ask yourself a lot of questions regarding your path forward:

- How much money do you need?
- How soon do you need it?
- Are there ways to earn money slowly over time and save up for it?
- How much do you have in savings?
- Are you okay with trading some ownership of your company in exchange for an investment?
- How important is it that the company remain 100 percent *yours*?
- Are you confident that you may be able to pay off interest?
- Are you currently in any debt right now?
- Is there a way to start this company off slower and grow to a more expensive way of operation over time? (For example, with Furever Home Friends, I started with print-on-demand in small quantities for the books before seeking out a large-scale printer.)

These are all questions that only YOU can answer about your business. This stage of business development requires you to analyze your own priorities within running a business and your own motivations for starting up your company. I also recommend seeking out the advice of a professional financial adviser, lawyer, accountant, or all three before making any huge financial commitments.

If you're in conversation with a banker or an investor, remember that while they might genuinely want to help your business succeed, they're also prioritizing their own interests above all else. Some bankers and investors are genuine people, but some only see dollar signs. While a deal might sound good on the surface, always remember to carefully map out and analyze all potential outcomes. And remember that you always have the power to negotiate with anyone, and that turning down an offer that isn't right for you is NEVER something to feel sorry about.

Deciding on a path to funding your business might not be easy. But you *can* do it! And if this all seems overwhelming right now, then don't worry: the next chapter is all about building a business on a budget!

8

Building a Business on a Budget

Here's a confession: I can be kind of a bitch. You probably noticed that in my introduction when I trashed other business books for their lack of specific advice, and then used that to elevate my own, as if this book I'm writing right now is somehow superior to other books that have been hitting the bestseller lists. But, contrary to popular belief, I don't just complain about things: I can also compliment something that's doing a job well.

I'm going to talk a little bit about a business book I read a couple years ago that inspired the heck out of me. That was *The Power of Broke* by Daymond John, founder of FUBU and investor on my aforementioned favorite reality TV show, *Shark Tank*. In this book, Daymond talks about how being broke doesn't have to be a death sentence for a business owner; actually, it can sometimes be an asset. He posits that having *less* money forces entrepreneurs to think of creative, cost-efficient solutions to problems that they wouldn't have had to think of had they had the money.

You know what? I think he's right. Sure, it's much easier to start a business if you've already got a million dollars just sitting in your bank account doing nothing. But in the long run, having to build a solid foundation on a tight budget can actually help your business develop strengths that you didn't even know it needed.

If I'd already had a ton of money available when I first started the Furever Home Friends, I would've never had to learn about crowdfunding. Crowdfunding forced me to publicize my business long before it was launched. It also helped me reach tons of people I'd never met before, friends of moms of friends of friends, and spread the word about the Furever Home Friends far and wide in just 30 days. If I had the money to travel to huge events in the first year and to pay for tables at giant conventions, I never would have forced myself to start off at small, local craft fairs and hone my sales skills in a lower-risk environment. Starting small and growing slowly allows us to learn along the way. And if I know one thing about business, it's that there are *so many* things to learn. I can't even imagine how much stuff is out there that I'm going to learn after I'm finished writing this book.

But one of the most valuable lessons I've learned over the past two years is how to start a business on a budget. We've already talked about ways to raise startup capital, so this chapter won't be about how to *raise* money for your business. Instead, these are my best tips for *saving* money while your business learns to take its first steps.

Work with Students

Let's get one thing clear before I start talking about working with students: you still have to pay them. As a small business owner, I'm a firm believer in paying *everyone* for their work. As you'll see in the section called "Barter" below, that doesn't always mean paying with money. But it does mean paying them in some way. (Side note: you are *not* allowed to make "exposure" your form of payment. If you're reading this book, you probably have a smaller audience than I do, and my exposure is basically worthless.) In fact, for this section, let's just assume you're going to pay all students you hire in cold, hard cash.

College students are often looking to build portfolios and beef up their resumes. Because they don't have decades of experience in the industry yet, they're often not charging the prices of someone who does.

But Savy!!! Why would I want to hire someone with a lack of experience? Well, that depends on your business. If your business produces medical equipment, then... well, maybe disregard this piece of advice. If your business requires employees to have certain licenses or certifications, then working with students may not be your best bet. But in some cases, students can be a wonderful asset.

When I started Furever Home Friends, my first two illustrators were college art students. Their work was beautiful. Let's be real: most people who devote their higher education to studying *art*, a very risky field, have some serious talent and dedication.

I interviewed a lot of illustrators at the beginning of the process. When I started my search for the perfect illustrators, I emailed a listserv for SCBWI (the Society of Children's Book Writers and Illustrators; I'll talk more about this organization in Chapter 11) and got responses from a multitude of interested artists. I also met one of my illustrators on an airplane, but again, you'll get that story in Chapter 11.

When evaluating the illustrators I was interviewing, I looked at three main components: 1) the quality of their artwork, 2) how well their art style fit with my business's branding and 3) how much they charged.

Notice that "how much they charged" was a point for evaluation, not for debate. You may already be a person who strongly believes in paying everyone you work with, but not everyone is that way. I got *so many questions* from people in my life about why I felt the need to pay the illustrators up front. Couldn't they take a royalty percentage? Couldn't I pay them per book sold? My answer to that was a big, hard NO. Furever Home Friends is *my* business. I own it. Unless an artist was planning to go into business with me and gain equity, I didn't feel right not paying them for a service. Also, having to pay royalties to multiple people every single month is a paperwork nightmare, and trust me, running a business is already enough of a paperwork nightmare—you don't need to make it worse.

Anyway, I weighed the quality and style of each artist's work along with their price. The artist who charged the least was a good artist, but her style didn't fully fit the look I was going for in my books. The artist who charged the most was a long-time industry professional with gorgeous work. However, two of the other illustrators, whose work was also gorgeous and fit my business's style, charged less than half of what she did.

I ended up hiring two illustrators, one for each of the first two books in the series. Both were art students at different colleges at the time. Hiring students was a win-win situation. I paid less than I would have paid for an artist with twenty years of professional experience, and they both made over two thousand dollars apiece, along with gaining book illustration experience to add to their portfolios and resumes.

There might be ways that you can hire students for your business as well. College kids studying marketing or public relations might be great for helping with your business's advertising. If you're not a writer, hiring an English major as a copywriter or editor may add a new strength to your business. They'll be giving you a lower-cost service in an area where you aren't as experienced, and you'll be giving them payment and industry experience.

Look Outside the Box for Resources

When you need to pay for a service for your business, it might seem like a good idea to just Google it. While that can work, sometimes there are cheaper (and even free!) resources available to you if you spend some time looking outside the box.

Here's an example. When entering the indie author world or starting up a book-related business, many people find themselves with a major expense on their plate: copyediting. For a complete novel, many good, experienced editors will charge rates in the thousands. However, I've never once paid an editor in my life. But every editor I've ever worked with *got paid*. How did I do this?

Well, this partially refers back to the previous point about working with students. But I did more than work with students at random schools that I found online or over email: I looked into the resources available at *my school*.

At DePaul University, where I got my Master's Degree in Writing & Publishing, there is a huge Writing Center. I know this because I worked there for two years. During my first year, I learned that one of the services the Writing Center offers is copyediting. Employees can sign up to be trained in copyediting for different styles (MLA, APA, Chicago, etc.) and then students, faculty, and alumni can submit complete, publication-ready projects for copyediting.

Both my new-adult novel *Sculpt Yourself* and my young-adult novel *One Final Vinyl* were edited by my co-workers at the Writing Center. They were paid hourly for their copyediting work. I got the service for free because I was a student (and now because I'm an alum). Their payment came from the school's Writing Center budget, which is there to provide resources like this to members of the school's community.

Not every school will have this option, however. But many colleges and universities have resources available to current students and to alumni, and you might not even know about them. When I've told other DePaul students how I've gotten two novels edited at the Writing Center, many of them had no idea that this was even an option. Even other students in my writing major! Sometimes, the best resources are hidden gems.

Barter! YES!

In my later chapter on networking, I discuss how I met and built a relationship with one of my greatest mentors and friends in the writing and publishing industry, a woman named Jan Spivey Gilchrist. At the time I'm writing this, Jan has had a forty-year-long illustrating career and has nearly a hundred children's books to her name. When I met her at a Chicago book fair in 2016, she quickly became my Book Industry Mom.

As I'm sure you can infer from my glowing description of her, Jan's illustration work is *gorgeous*. When I was working on the fourth Furever Home Friends book, I was hoping that I could finally get to work with some of her beautiful art.

One problem: since Jan was (and still is) an incredibly experienced industry veteran, there would be *no way* I could afford her prices. One solution: I worked with Jan as an editor for a few books she was working on. That meant we had the opportunity to trade services, or to engage in the classic practice of bartering.

A lot of people seem to think bartering as a form of exchange is dead. I have to disagree. Sure, maybe we don't regularly trade our best goat to marry the neighbor's daughter anymore—and thank goodness for that—but that doesn't mean that money *has* to always be your only form of currency.

Jan and I made an agreement that I would edit her next complete book in exchange for her doing all of the illustrations for the fourth Furever Home Friends book, *Kringle's Christmas.* We each had a skill that the other person required at the time: thus, a bartering relationship was born.

Now, will opportunities to barter appear around every corner? Probably not. It's *much* easier to get a service you want by paying for it. But if you have absolutely no money to spend on that service, I recommend looking for places where you can trade. If you need a website designed, see if any of the web designers you know are currently looking to fill a need that you can provide.

Disclaimer: this does *not* mean that it's okay to trade someone "exposure" or "experience" in exchange for their hard work. Unless you're a celebrity with millions of followers and fans, your publicity will *not* be worth their time financially. However, if you have an actual *good or service* you can trade them, then I say, go for it!

Part 3

The Business

Exists!

Now What?

9

Goal-Setting Basics

Let's get a little meta.

My goal is to get this book out by my 28th birthday. My first step in that process is to finish writing it. My goal to finish writing this book is to reach the end of draft one during NaNoWriMo 2019, which ends November 30th. While I'm currently writing this sentence, it is November 17th, and I still have a ways to go. That means that my goal for tonight is to write for the next hour, until I've gotten down about 1,000 more words, no matter how badly I want to head into the living room to play tug-of-war with Chewie or some Nintendo Switch games with Tyler.

It would be awfully easy to say, "Well, I want to get this book out by my 28th birthday, which is in

September of 2020. I'm currently typing this sentence in November of 2019, which means I have plenty of time, so I don't need to set any more goals for this." But for me, that type of thinking can cause me to fall behind and decrease in productivity.

It's no secret that starting a business is a *big* goal. If running your own business were easy, everyone would do it. Isn't that the dream? To do what you love, set your own hours, and have no boss? If so, why doesn't everyone do it? Oh yeah, because it's *hard* and requires not just a ton of day-to-day work, but also a *metric butt-load* of planning and forethought.

Right now, I have a goal to have 15 total books published before I'm 30 years old. At the time of typing this sentence, I have recently turned 27 and have 6 books published. By the time I turn 28, I plan to have 8 total books published, including this one. However, if I stopped my goal-setting there, I would wake up on my thirtieth birthday and wonder where the time went—and as someone with OCD that leads to regular existential crises… that would *not* be a good feeling. Instead, I'm using a five-year planner right now to map out my goals for each month between now (again, November 2019) and the end of 2023.

For me, staying productive throughout every step of business has come from my ability to set large goals, break them down into smaller goals, and frequently revise the steps needed to accomplish each new milestone.

In this chapter, I'm going to share some of my best practices for setting giant, intimidating goals, figuring out *how* to complete them, and executing my big plan. Let's make it happen!

Start with the Big Picture!

Working backwards, in my experience, is the best way to set a goal and identify all the sub-goals residing within it. If you're planning something big, like starting a new business, I'd go so far as to say it's a necessity to start with the big picture. If you don't know what your end goal is — your business's mission, your products, etc. — how can you figure out the steps to achieve those things?

I started with a big-picture goal for myself: *I want to write and publish a series of books and plushies based on real rescue dogs.* This goal has *so* many smaller goals within it, from the goal of finishing the first draft of the first book, to the goal of putting in a bulk order for 600 stuffed animals. However, without knowing how I wanted my business to be structured and what I wanted it to look like, it would've been impossible to determine what smaller goals I should set and what steps I should take to achieve them.

When I have a lot of big goals, I like to brainstorm. The process of brainstorming can be really fun. You can make it interactive and tactile, and then it starts to feel like less of a chore.

At the beginning of a new year, I like to brainstorm my yearly goals by breaking out my bullet journal, drawing a giant box in the middle of the first page, and sectioning it off with some shiny washi tape. Shiny washi tape is optional for brainstorming, of course; but for me, it feels like I'm doing arts and crafts, not business strategizing. I also like to write the "BRAINSTORMING" in big, puffy bubble letters at the top of the page.

Then, I set a timer on my phone. I give myself five minutes to write down EVERY big goal that I can think of for the year. Do I want to publish a new book? Do I want to sell 20 percent more than I sold in the previous year? Do I want to get my business on the radio or on TV? Do I want my YouTube channel to gain 5,000 subscribers? Write as many big goals as you can before that piercing high-pitched ring erupts from your phone to let you know that time's up. Then, look at all the goals you wrote and choose a few to start breaking down.

Break it into Steps!

Each big goal has many smaller goals living inside of it. A goal is like a Russian nesting doll, or like one of those big boxes people give you on Christmas as a gag gift, only to find that there's actually twelve other boxes inside, and the real gift is like a piece of candy or something. (Was that just my family?)

There are two ways I like to break down my goals: **by sub-goal and by timeframe**. In the next few sections, we'll talk about how to break it down by time. Before I even think about giving myself deadlines, though, I need to figure out each step residing inside each small goal residing in each big goal.

For example, when I first conceived the idea for Furever Home Friends, starting my business was my big goal. Within that goal were a few smaller goals: writing the first two books, getting the books illustrated, designing the stuffed animals, getting the first run of the books printed, and, *of course*, finding the *money* to do all of this!

I then took each of those smaller goals and broke them into steps. Here's how that looks:

MAJOR GOAL: START A BUSINESS CALLED "THE FUREVER HOME FRIENDS"

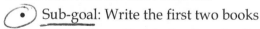 Sub-goal: Write the first two books
- o Step: Finish the first draft of *Princess Allee* and *Smile, Chewie!*
- o Step: Take these drafts to my critique group and get feedback.

- o Step: Rewrite both drafts (probably three or so times).

- Sub-goal: Get the books illustrated
  - o Step: Find an illustrator for each book; reach out to artists I know, art groups online, and email listservs. Review the work each illustrator sends as a sample and compare the quality with the price they're asking. Offer the position to two illustrators.
  - o Step: Make a contract regarding payment, deadlines, and intellectual property rights. Send this to the illustrators, get them to sign it, and file the signed version away in a folder for business documents.
  - o Step: Break down the manuscripts for each book into 24 sections, one for each page. Send the breakdown to the illustrators so they know what to draw for each page.
  - o Step: Receive illustrations and work on book formatting.

- Sub-goal: Design stuffed animals
  - o Step: Work with my mom to design a sewing pattern.
  - o Step: Use the pattern and scrap fabric to make mock-ups of the plush. Adjust design based on what works.

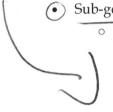

- o Step: Buy bulk sheets of flannel in the right colors for the dogs.
- Sub-goal: Get books printed
  - o Research the per-book costs in various quantities for various printing services like CreateSpace, IngramSpark, BookBaby, Lulu, and more.
  - o Choose a service and set up an account.
  - o Upload book files to the printing site.
  - o Order proofs of the books at least a month before the scheduled release date.
  - o Make any necessary adjustments and order another proof.
  - o Once the proof looks correct, put in a bulk order for 200 books.
- Sub-goal: Find the money to do all of this
  - o Before I do anything else, set up a Kickstarter page.
  - o Do all necessary calculations to figure out the *bare minimum* amount I'd need to raise to make this a reality.
  - o Film and edit a video for the Kickstarter page.
  - o Launch and publicize the page (using all the techniques discussed in the Crowdfunding chapter).

o   Schedule all release dates based on the date money will be received (generally about two weeks after the campaign ends).

Even the steps to each of these goals can have *other* steps hidden inside of them. Big goals are like a giant Pandora's box. Except instead of demons, what's hiding inside is *a butt-load of more work*. That's why it's important not just to break down each goal into steps, but also to break each goal down by time, from what *year* you want something accomplished, to what you'll do *each day* to work towards it.

Break it Down by Year

Remember when I said I like to use a five-year planner? That's because, when I have *big goals* stuffed full of smaller goals stuffed full of individual steps, which are stuffed full of *even smaller steps*, I need to plan things way ahead. I need to know what I want to accomplish in each year, which month each thing should be accomplished by, where I should be each week to be on track for that, and what tasks I need to accomplish daily.

I use three planners at the same time: my physical five-year planner to break down goals by year, my Google calendar to break goals down by month and week, and a daily planner to create to-do lists.

Now, Break it Down by Month!

Within each month, there should be goals that you need to accomplish to progress toward the bigger yearly goal. Let me be clear: breaking things down by year or by month does not mean that you have to set specific goals to be accomplished between January and December, and then specific goals for the 1st-31st of the month. Sometimes you might accomplish something big on the 12th of the month, or one of your big yearly goals in March.

When you break your goals down by month, it can be helpful to use a big monthly calendar with a block for each day. I do NOT use these calendars to write daily tasks, appointment reminders, or schedules. Instead, I write in very large handwriting and set *deadlines*. So, if I have a big calendar of the month of April in front of me, and my goal is to launch my Kickstarter page by April 7 and finish my first draft of a book by April 20, I will write those goals' deadlines REALLY BIG in that day's box. In the empty days *between* goal deadlines, I can now visually see the amount of time I have to accomplish it.

Now, Break it Down by Week!

This is where Google Calendar has been my friend. I love Google Calendar's weekly views on my desktop computer screen and on my phone. Of course, if you're a Mac user, iCalendar works as well, and so does any similar online calendar program.

For my Google calendar, I break goals down by week. The first thing I do is physically block out the obligations I have in any given week and color-code them. So, if I have to go into work to teach a creative writing workshop, that's green (for MONEY!). If I have to conduct interviews for an article I'm writing, I schedule those in red. Then, I add in other things, like showering and eating, in yellow. Yellow is my "personal maintenance" color. A lot of people think it's silly that I schedule my showers, my meals, and my reminders to do the dishes and laundry. But if you knew me when I was just starting this business, going to school, and working 90+ hour weeks, then you probably knew how bad I smelled, how much mold was in my sink, and how inexplicably tired I was because all I had to eat was tortilla chips in between classes. So, yes, I *do* need to schedule those things.

After I've blocked in all the pre-scheduled necessities, it's time for me to block out times to accomplish each goal for the week. For example, if one of my monthly goal deadlines was to have a book draft written by a certain date, I might schedule 2 hours a day in the week leading up to it to work on it.

Blocking out time to accomplish goals throughout the week helps me keep a balance on how much I'm doing. However, when it comes to goals that aren't scheduled with other people, I notice that I sometimes need to shift up the order that I accomplish them, or sometimes need to break down smaller steps within each one. That's when my daily planner comes in.

Finally, Break it Down by Day!

At the time I started writing this first draft, my "daily planner" was a hodgepodge of Post-It notes on my desk. I stuck them to the edges of my computer monitor, I stuck them under my keyboard, I stuck them right in front of where I sit, and, when I was done with that day's post it note, I would throw it in the trash can under my desk. Of course, if you know me, you know I have *no aim,* which means that more often than not, the space underneath my desk would be a giant leaf pile of used Post-It notes.

Over the last few months, though, I started using a daily planner. The one I use is from Clever Fox, which I highly recommend, because they make planners where you can break down daily goals, sub-goals, priorities, to-do lists, and schedules. However, I've also heard that other planner brands are great as well, so definitely shop around!

When I plan daily, I sit down and write out a to-do list for the day based on the goals blocked out on my Google Calendar. So, going with the earlier example of finishing a book draft, if I were to set aside two hours a day to work on writing that book, then one of my to-do list items would be "write for 2 hours" or "write 2,000 words" or "reach the end of x chapter." I also fill my to-do lists with necessities, like cooking, showering, sleeping, eating, and cleaning up.

Daily to-do lists can also help break down larger goals for the day. So, for example, if one of my time blocks in the Google Calendar says "edit videos," I might make a to-do list with a sub-list of all the videos I need to get done that day. I might also include smaller steps like uploading the video to YouTube and scheduling it for a premiere.

I *always* draw check boxes next to my to-do list items! For me, the act of checking off a box gives me a tactile reward for the accomplishment. I'm not a psychologist, so take what I'm saying here with a grain of salt, but I feel like engaging different parts of your body in a task—even in small ways, like checking off a box when a task is done—increases that inner feeling of accomplishment.

I know that everyone's goal-setting process is different. If you try setting goals and using multiple planners like I do, maybe you'll end up even more stressed and overwhelmed than before. I encourage you to try different methods and find one that you're excited to stick with. (Literally *stick* with, in my case; what got me on the planner-using hype train was that I could put stickers in my planner. STICKERS, GUYS!)

No matter what your planning method or process is, keep in mind that strong, actionable goals have both long-term and short-term parts, and *all* of the goals involved, both large and small, need to be identified in order to stay on track. Now, go set some goals!

10

Let's Get Logistical!

When I finally decided what to title this chapter, I suddenly got Olivia Newton-John singing "Let's Get Physical!" stuck in my head. Fun fact: that was my favorite song in high school. Both because I had a weird obsession with the 80s for a teenager in 2009, and because I liked to make puns out of it in physics class. But guess what? This isn't a physics book. So we're not going to get physical. Instead, we're going to get logistical!

"When you start a small business to do the thing you're passionate about, you end up spending so little time on that compared to what you spend on logistics." That's what a fellow business owner told me shortly after I started Furever Home Friends. This person owned one of the first stores to

130

carry our products, and I was there to conduct a book signing. She was telling me how she opened up a store to sell her original work since she loved graphic design and screen-printing. While she still got to do that, she didn't originally realize just how much time was going to be spent on market research, spreadsheets, budgets, and more.

So, in this chapter, we're going to talk about those things! Let's get ready to … get *logistical!*

Your Business Plan

Just like you map out your own goals, you should map out your goals for your business as a whole. As we discussed in the Goal-Setting chapter, these goals should cover the big picture as well as all the small steps you need to take to get there. To plot out all of these goals, I recommend writing a business plan. Your business plan might only be a few pages long, or it might be 50 pages or more. It all depends on how much research you need to do and how detailed you want to get before starting. When mapping out your business plan, I recommend breaking it into sections such as Business Model, Market Research, and Finance. Even if you don't have to present a formal business plan or proposal to potential investors, it can still be useful to open up a document and start writing out all of these pieces of your plan in one place.

Business Model

Before you start operating, one of the most important things to decide is what business model you're going to use. *How* will you make money?

For Furever Home Friends, my business model is fairly simple: sales. I sell products to customers. Sometimes, I sell inventory to stores, but the end goal is sales. Not every business will work this way, however.

For example, maybe your business idea is an app or a mobile game. Many apps are free to download, so if you try to charge users for your program, you might lose customers to competitors. So, maybe you need to use a different business model, such as ad revenue. In that case, instead of figuring out how to get customers to give you their money, you'll be thinking of ways to partner with other companies to run ads on your program.

Maybe you do sell products directly to customers, but instead of selling individual products, you want to start a monthly subscription. Maybe you're going to start a magazine that customers receive monthly. Maybe you want to start a curated box of items that monthly subscribers can receive, such as a monthly book or wine club. In that case, your business model will require you to retain customers over a longer period as well as build relationships with brands whose products you want to sell.

If the model you want to choose is multilevel marketing, go back to Chapter Three and read it again.

It's also possible that you might not know what model you want your business to follow yet. For example, maybe you want to start a video production company. Well, you can use many different models for that. Do you want to make independent movies that you sell to consumers as DVDs? Do you want to make movies that you enter into festivals to win prizes? Do you want to create free YouTube videos that earn ad revenue through Google? Do you want to create free YouTube videos that don't earn ad revenue, but do convince people to go to your website and pay for higher production value videos? Or maybe you want to produce videos for other people. Maybe you want to offer a filming or editing service to companies who need videos made about their products. Or maybe you want to offer filming or editing services to young couples who want cute wedding videos.

The possibilities may seem endless. If you're not sure which specific model you want to go with yet, try writing about all of them! See what ideas come to mind. Brainstorm how you might make money in each potential situation. It will be crucial to nail down your model before you begin operating, but it's fine to explore different options as you write out a business plan.

Market Research

Regardless of your industry, it's important to know what else is already out there and how you're going to be both similar and different. I talked about this topic earlier in the book; realizing that my business functioned similar to a company like American Girl was helpful for determining my competitors.

For me, defining other businesses in my market came with a bit of insecurity. *If there's already a business like mine, does that mean I'm not original?* Well, we all know that in this day and age, pretty much *nothing* is truly original. And there's nothing wrong with that! I wasn't going to be the first children's book author, or the first stuffed animal and toy company, or even the first company to sell a combination of the two. But I was going to do it in my own way!

When determining your industry, competitors, and target customer, it can be helpful to break some of these vague concepts into hard numbers. When completing market research for your business, try to answer the following questions as specifically as possible.

- Who do I want to buy my products, subscribe to my service, view my content, etc.?
- How old is that target audience member?
- Does my business's output skew more toward a particular demographic: gender, marital status, cultural background, etc.?
- Does my business serve a specific location? Do I want to start by serving a specific town or city and then expand, or do I want to serve everyone online at once?
- How many consumers in my target demographic or location are looking for a product like mine? For example, if you want to open a burger restaurant, you might look up how many people in your town are searching for burger restaurants using sites like Google or Yelp.
- Who are my biggest competitors? Who sells products like mine or offers a similar service?
- How much do my biggest competitors sell? How many customers do they have? How many products do they sell annually? What is their annual revenue?

By analyzing how your competitors are doing, you can also determine the demand for your product or service. Like I talked about earlier, one of the most basic principles of business—and one we probably all heard about ad nauseum in a high school social studies class—is supply and demand. Is there a big demand out there for what you're offering right now? Do you offer something that people want, and what numbers do you have to back that up?

Now, what if the answer is no? What if after all this research, you determine that there just aren't that many people searching for burger restaurants in your town, or that the industry you want to enter is suffering? Well, you have a few options.

First, you could choose a different business model. That might sound discouraging, especially if you were really excited about the specific business you had planned. But you also have another option: choose to operate on a small scale. Find a way to operate your business in a low-cost, low-output way that still brings you revenue. It might not be the level of revenue you were originally hoping to earn, but it might be the best option until that industry is ready for more companies to enter.

For example, if I needed to scale down Furever Home Friends, I could stop selling stuffed animals, signed books, and 3D printed toys on my website, and instead choose to sell books printed on demand through a site like Amazon's KDP or merch printed on demand through Printful or RedBubble. This would not be the ideal business for me, but that is always an option I have if my industry starts to suffer.

Finance

As cool as it would be if businesses were about passion or creativity or love, the truth is, at the end of the day... businesses are about *money*. That's not to say they can't *also* be about passion and creativity and love—hey, look at how much my INCREDIBLE LOVE FOR DOGS and my INSANE PASSION FOR BOOKS inspired my business—but without the monetary component, there's nothing separating your business from a hobby.

Because money is important to a business, it's important that, when you're planning out your business, you start running some hard numbers at the beginning.

Here are some financial questions I'd recommend you ask yourself before launching your first product or service:

 What are all the things I need to start this business, and how much will those things cost? More specific sub-questions about this topic might include:

 Am I planning to register my business as a sole proprietorship, partnership, LLC, or corporation?

What are my state's filing fees to register my business?

Do I need to purchase any new equipment to start my business (for example, a laptop, a camera, a microphone, a specific software program for your computer, a sewing machine, etc.) and how much does that equipment cost?

Do I need to purchase materials to create samples or prototypes of my products? How much does that cost?

(If you're selling physical products) What is the minimum bulk order I need to put in for my first run of products, and how much will that cost? Have I shopped around with different manufacturers? What is the difference in price and product quality?

Do I need to hire any employees to start, or will I be doing everything myself? If I need to hire employees, how much total will that cost? If I'm planning to run everything myself, will I have any contract employees like an accountant or lawyer that I'll pay as needed? How much should I budget for that?

How much do I intend to charge for each product? (Or, if you're running a service-based business or freelance business, how much do you intend to charge per hour of work or per completed assignment?)

How much do other products in my industry tend to cost? For this, I recommend going on Amazon or a similar site, finding the top 100 best-selling products in your category, and taking the average and median of the prices you find. For example, I might look up the 100 best-selling children's books in the "Dog" category on Amazon, add up the prices of all these books, and divide by 100.

Should I charge less than the average and have my low prices be a selling point? Or can I charge a bit more than the average and justify it with another aspect of my product—such as it being handmade, durable, or high quality—be the selling point instead.

Even if you are selling a service rather than a physical product, you can still use this technique. When I first started working as a freelance copyeditor, I searched for other editors' prices and saw what most people were charging. I decided to charge more than most of the editors I found on Fiverr because I prioritized building a personal, long-lasting relationship with my clients rather than trying to get a ton of clients at once.

If your business plans look anything like mine, they'll be *filled* with math! If you see numbers, multiplication signs, and more all over your document, you're probably doing something right!

Logistical Logging

You can't spell *logistics* without *log*. I'm not here to discuss etymology, though, so I can't tell you with any kind of authority whether that is intentional. What *needs* to be intentional, though, is how you *log* every single expense your business incurs and every bit of revenue your business makes.

One of the easiest ways to fall behind in business is not to track all your expenses.

The most common reasons I've found, based on my own experiences and stories others have told me (so this is all anecdotal evidence, not hard statistics), that people neglect to log everything for their business are:

- Stress: When you're feeling overwhelmed, it's easy to fall back on the tasks that feel the least stressful. For many of us, filling out a spreadsheet with costs and revenue isn't the fun part of running a business. If you feel too stressed to do your spreadsheet today, write yourself a note reminding yourself to fill it out on another day this week. Block out a half hour to *get it done!*

- Frustration: If math isn't your strong suit, it might feel like a major chore to fill in your spreadsheet, even if you're using functions so the document calculates for you. I get it, though; it can feel really frustrating to keep working with a program or skill that isn't usual for your business. I wish I had a cool hack or trick to make this less frustrating, but the truth is, I don't. I just tell myself to bite the bullet and do it. Sometimes I play 90s grunge music in the background to feel inspired.

- Denial: Sometimes, we want to tell ourselves our business is doing better than it is. We always hear how important it is to have an optimistic mindset and to stay positive. In some cases, the easiest way to stay positive is by only thinking about your positive revenue. But that's an incredibly destructive way to view business. If you just look at the deposits going into your bank account from your credit card reader or from your customers' Paypals, it can get addictive to see that amount in your bank account increase, and to ignore the withdrawals for expenditures. It can be hard to write down all the exact amounts that you spent on things and see in black and white that you didn't make much legitimate profit this month. But it is *necessary* to know.

In fact, for everyone who's new, let's just take a minute to distinguish between revenue and profit.

- <u>Revenue</u> is the amount of money your business is bringing in. It's a great way to see how many sales you're actually making or how much money you're generating overall. However, revenue does not show how much *you made*, and it is not an indicator of how profitable your business currently is.
- <u>*Profit*</u> is revenue *minus expenditures*. If you brought in $10,000 this year, but you spent $20,000 on products, advertisements, licenses, fees, etc., then your business did not make a profit—that's what businesses mean when they say they're *in the red*. However, that doesn't mean your business is never going to make a profit; it just means you

might have to adjust your production for the following year. But it's important to know exactly how much *revenue and profit* you're bringing in monthly and yearly.

Spreadsheets are Excellent! *yes!!!*

That was a pun. Get it? They're Excel-lent. Because you likely use Microsoft Excel. (This book was not sponsored by Microsoft. Plus, actually, I use Google Sheets. But if you didn't come to this book for the Dad Jokes, why are you even here?)

I use spreadsheets so much right now. In fact, my business spreadsheet is open on the tab *directly next to* the tab where I'm writing this! While the importance of spreadsheets may seem obvious to some of my fellow spreadsheet lovers out there, I know it's not obvious to everyone, so for those of you who don't use spreadsheets, I am here to sell you on the joy of them.

Spreadsheets can do *so much math!* Whether you love or hate doing math, the amount of constant addition and subtraction that business requires can get old after a while. While it might seem easy to just keep a list in a Word document of all your expenses and your earnings, using a spreadsheet can let you add everything up and even run different equations to predict future revenue.

Spreadsheets feel like magic to me. When I add in all my sales figures from a new event or from the last month of online orders, I get to watch that "revenue for the year" number rise—and the satisfaction of it never falters.

If you're not already well versed in spreadsheets, my best advice to you is to learn how to use functions. Learn where you need to add a sum function and where you need to subtract items. Learn how to add up multiple cells throughout the spreadsheet.

Of course, spreadsheets aren't always fun and games. They can break your heart sometimes. But in business, heartbreak is necessary for growth.

The heartbreak I'm talking about here is your *business expenses spreadsheet*. While I'd love to track only the money I bring in, it's equally important to track the money going OUT. You need to log EVERY business expense on your spreadsheet!

My recommendation is to make an Excel or Google Sheets file with multiple tabs. Make one tab of your spreadsheet for revenue and another for expenses. When all your math is done, bolden or highlight your total revenue number on one sheet and your total expense number on the other. That way, it will be easy to compare how much you've spent versus how much you've earned.

To many readers right now, this point might sound obvious. But I've known too many people who didn't track their expenses thoroughly and had a false sense of how much profit their business is bringing in.

In the same vein, it's important to remember the difference between revenue and profit. A quick reminder, in case you forgot what I said two pages ago: revenue is how much *total* money your business has brought in; profit is how much you've earned *minus expenses*.

When I say to make sure you're logging all your business expenses, I mean *all* of them! Did you pay a fee to attend a business networking event? Add it into your spreadsheet. Did you spend $5 on a short-term Facebook ad campaign? Log it in your spreadsheet. Did you spend $20 for an hour consulting with a potential social media manager, only later to decide you don't want to hire one long-term? Still, log that $20 in your spreadsheet!

Beyond keeping yourself aware of how your business is actually doing, logging your expenses will also help you come tax season. If you logged *all* your expenses, your net profit won't be artificially inflated; that means less income you'll pay tax on!

Now, I am NOT an accountant, and I do NOT give professional tax advice. Make sure to talk thoroughly with an accountant before figuring out the best way to file your taxes for your business. But I *will* say, this is not an opportunity to abuse the system. Some people might say, "Oh, if I log ALL my expenses and have a lower net profit, I don't have to pay as much in taxes? Well… I ate breakfast this morning, and food was necessary for me to have the energy to do my work, so I'm going to log ALL my grocery expenses! I need electricity to run my business, so I'll write off my ENTIRE electric bill, including the electricity used to watch TV!" Don't do that. You might risk getting audited, and no one wants to go through an audit.

For some business owners, logistics aren't the fun part. We're here to create new products! To connect with customers! To offer a life-changing product or service! Not to do MATH all day! Well, if you've done your math correctly, and you find that you have extra room in your budget… then hey, maybe you can hire someone to manage your spreadsheets *for* you!

But until then… let's get LOGISTICAL together!

11

Networking:
My Favorite (and Only) Hobby!

I used to have exactly one hobby: music. Here, I'm defining *hobby* as an activity that you're passionate about, but never intend to do for money. Until I was about 22 years old, playing music had been a lifelong hobby for me.

Music was one of my only passions that I never seriously considered as a career path. Writing was never a hobby; since early childhood I knew I wanted to write professionally. Video games were never a hobby. I never cared if I won or lost, if I played well or sucked; they were more of a stress-relieving, passive activity for me. The only activity that I ever practiced, joined groups for, and genuinely *cared about*, all with no intent to pursue it professionally, was music. Throughout middle school, high school, and college, I played the bassoon and the alto saxophone. I spent four years in a competitive high-school marching band and the following four years in a Big Ten Division I college marching band.

Outside of marching band practice, football games, orchestra rehearsals, and playing with my sorority's jazz combo, I worked my *ass off* on my other career goals. I spent every second of free time writing novels and screenplays. I took as many art classes as I could and I worked on my drawing, painting, and digital art skills. I took economics classes and tried out miniature versions of businesses, such as putting up an Etsy page or designing a greeting card line. But through it all, I was always at marching band practice on time, and I was always ready to play my saxophone.

And wouldn't you know it? It wasn't *any* of my classes or my side projects or my failed business ventures that secured my first paid writing job. It was music.

When I was a senior in college, the marching band's alumni group decided to try out a mentorship program that paired seniors with alumni in their chosen field. I filled out their survey, explained that my career goals all lay in writing, and I soon received my match: a woman named

Christine who graduated from Northwestern 17 years prior, played flute in the marching band back in the 90s, and was the editor-in-chief of a music publication called *Halftime Magazine*.

After getting to know her over our scheduled mentorship phone calls, I asked her about the opportunity to write for *Halftime*. She had me write a short article as a trial, and within a month, I was hired as a feature journalist. At my time of writing this sentence (November 2019, in case you weren't listening the first ten million times I mentioned that), I have been working for *Halftime* as a writer for four years. Two months ago, I was promoted to assistant editor. I have also gotten to know my mentor-turned-boss, Christine, really well. She came to my wedding. We've traveled to band-related events together. Gaining her as a mentor led to one of the most rewarding professional relationships of my work life so far.

And all of this made me realize something. It wasn't *only* music that gained me this job. It was also *networking*.

Nowadays, I have exactly zero hobbies. In my experience, running a business leaves no room for leisure activities, at least those with any sort of learning curve (there's a reason all my favorite video games are targeted at middle schoolers). It was a bittersweet realization; I was both pursuing my passion as my full-time work, turning my hobbies into a career, and also working so many hours that I had no time to pursue any interests *outside* of my career field.

Along the way, though, I adopted a new saying: "Networking is my favorite hobby!" Now, this completely goes against the way I defined a *hobby* at the beginning of the chapter. Networking is never something I did *solely* for fun; it was always to expand my connections as an entrepreneur. But by recontextualizing the concept of "networking" in my brain as a hobby, I was able to see it not as a chore or obligation, but rather as a new spin on a fun activity I already loved: meeting new people with similar interests and making new friends. After all, my one lifelong hobby, music, is what caused me to believe in the power of networking in the first place.

In 2016, before the Furever Home Friends was even a twinkle in my first crowdfunding campaign's eye, I made another important connection through networking, which ended up benefiting my future business in remarkable ways.

I had joined Chicago's chapter of the Society of Children's Book Writers & Illustrators (SCBWI) to meet other writers and make new writer friends. At the time, I was mostly looking for critique groups for my YA novels. My first YA novella, *Beauty King*, had just recently released, and my YA novel *One Final Vinyl* (which, at the time of this book's publication, should be released as well!) was in its first drafting stage. Though I was mostly looking to meet other YA authors, I also had this draft of a picture book called *Princess Allee* that I'd been revising on and off for the past six or seven years, and I wanted to meet other who could help me figure out what to do with it. (Spoiler: I figured out what to do with it. It was the Furever Home Friends. But if you're reading this book in order, that was probably obvious to you already.)

Every year, a store called 57th Street Books hosts a children's literature festival on the South Side of Chicago, and SCBWI frequently has a table there. In 2016, shortly after I'd joined, everyone got an email requesting that we staff the table for an hour at the festival. I was excited to go to the festival, so I signed up for an hour in the morning.

When I got to Nichols Park for the festival, everything was, for lack of a better term, *whimsical*. Balloons were everywhere. Kids' dance companies performed routines on a little stage. Children's authors had tables set up all throughout a grassy field. Everything was colorful, bright, and happy. I found the SCBWI table and took a seat next to a fellow author who had the same shift I did.

During our hour staffing the table, I somehow got on the topic of freelance editing, and how I was planning to start copyediting for a few clients. As a lifelong grammar nerd, it seemed like the perfect side-hustle.

Instead of just nodding and smiling, like most people did when I talked about my passion for punctuation, the lady next to me said, "Oh, have you met Jan? I think she's looking for an editor!"

Well, at this point, I'd been out of college for a full year, and I *knew* what the power of networking could do for me! So naturally, I went to find Jan.

Jan's table was like nothing I could have ever expected: she had racks and racks set up next to it, full of a variety of books, all filled with gorgeous, lifelike illustrations. Here I was, walking up to Jan's table, thinking I was just about to make a new friend, completely unaware that I was about to introduce myself to Jan Spivey Gilchrist, one of the most renowned children's illustrators in Chicago, winner of the Coretta Scott King Award, and artist for over 90 books.

It's probably a good thing I was so oblivious, because instead of getting star-struck, I just walked up to her table and said, "Hi, are you Jan? Someone told me you're looking for a new editor."

Thankfully, Jan was one of the *friendliest* people I'd ever met. She told me that yes, she was specifically looking for a young person to work with. She was about 70, and I had just turned 24 a few days earlier. She told me that she wanted a millennial because she wanted to work with someone who had a different perspective on the world than she did and who saw technology in a different way.

I gave her my card. She gave me her phone number.

Guess what? Jan also became one of my best friends. I edited her manuscripts. She came to my book launch parties. I went to movie premieres and dinner with her. Just like Christine, she came to my wedding.

Jan became one of the most important connections in my network—not only from the joy of making a wonderful new friend, but also for my business. When I was finishing up the manuscript for the fourth Furever Home Friends book, *Kringle's Christmas*, I decided to reach out to Jan as an illustrator. I'd always thought her art was gorgeous, and like I mentioned earlier, I wanted to have a different illustrator for every book.

However, I was tight on money, especially since I was trying to save up for bulk production of the stuffed animals. That's when I decided to use the bartering technique, which I talked about in the "Building a Business on a Budget" chapter. I traded Jan my editing services for her books in exchange for her illustrations in mine. I ended up with a beautiful Christmas book and an even more beautiful friendship—all thanks to the power of networking!

So, what are my best tips for networking?

Carry a Business Card Everywhere

Yeah, I can totally be That Bitch™ at parties sometimes. Or That Bro™ if you think I give off more of the frat-bro-business-major type of vibes. But I've been caught *without* a business card in situations where I'd need them enough times to know it's a good idea to carry a business card *everywhere*. I bought a small business-card holder on Amazon—small enough to slide into my front pocket, even in those women's skinny jeans that have the saddest, most fraudulent excuses for pockets you've ever seen. I pack it with business cards, slide it into my pocket, and carry it with me everywhere.

Join a Group or Society!

One of the best investments I ever made—well, other than my brief childhood foray into the stock market—was a simple $125 payment to join my neighborhood's Chamber of Commerce. Since Chicago is *huge*, we have a Chamber of Commerce for individual neighborhoods, but if you live in a smaller town or city, your town/city might have its own Chamber as well.

I first found the Chamber of Commerce at a tent at RibFest. I think RibFest might also be just a

Chicago (and surrounding Chicago suburbs) thing. But it's this big festival where everyone sets up giant tents and huge barbecue restaurants from all over the country gather to sell their ribs (and chicken and pulled pork and stuff). There are bands playing and vendors throughout the fairground. (Well, I say fairground, but if you live in the city like me, it's more of a blocked off street. In the burbs, though, it's a field.) I was planning to sell Furever Home Friends books and plushies at RibFest 2020, except... well, we all know what happened to 2020.

Anyway, while I was at RibFest, hoping to find out some more information about securing a spot there as a vendor for the following year (again, as I was blissfully unaware that Corona was anything other than a mediocre summer beer), I came across a tent for the Chamber of Commerce. I took some of their pamphlets and learned what the group was about: networking! As soon as I learned I would get to network with all the other awesome small business owners in my neighborhood, I was *so there*.

Shortly after I registered with the Chamber, the president emailed me to set up a meeting. We met at a coffee shop a block from my house and discussed my business's goals. He gave me an hour of professional one-on-one advice to figure out not only how I could use the Chamber's services, but how I would fit into the dynamic of all these businesses helping each other.

He helped me find contact information for businesses in the neighborhood I could partner with—like day-care centers where I could do an author visit and book reading, or upcoming events where I could be a vendor. He helped me brainstorm ideas for other ways I could partner with the businesses in the neighborhood. Because this initial meeting took place back when I was still deciding whether I might want to pursue a business loan, he helped direct me toward private, local lenders for consultations.

Running any kind of business isn't just about you and your customers. It's also about how you can collaborate. For those of you who found me on YouTube, many of you have commented or messaged me to say that you found me from one of my collab videos with another creator you watched. I've also had some of my viewers—those who have been there since I began YouTube in late 2018—who've told me about new channels they LOVE that they've discovered through guests on my channel. Collaborating and partnering with other businesses is exactly the same: you form a mutually beneficial relationship with another entrepreneur and both of you find new audiences.

In November of 2019, I was scrambling. It was almost time for the 2nd Annual Happy

Pawlidays Party, but I'd completely slacked off on promotion. (Well, *slacked off* might just be me once again being too hard on myself; more like, I became overwhelmed with the constant holiday events, promotions, sales, and special items I was offering.)

The Happy Pawlidays Party is an annual event I created at the end of 2018. The event was initially intended to be a launch party for our fourth book, *Kringle's Christmas*, but it ended up turning into something more: an animal shelter fundraiser combined with a book signing. The 2018 event had been huge: I'd partnered with ALIVE Rescue, the shelter where real-life Kringle was from, and Jan Spivey Gilchrist, the award-winning illustrator of the book was there signing books for customers. I wrote press releases months in advance and sent them to local news sources. I completely sold out of *Kringle's Christmas* that day. It was magical.

2019's Pawliday Party wasn't starting off so well. Due to scheduling conflicts, the party had to be the weekend before Thanksgiving, and I'd just been starting my holiday events at that point. I'd finalized my holiday display—a cute snowy scene with plushies of Allee and Kringle (wearing puffy coats and boots) sliding down a hill (made of white foam) on a miniature sled together, while Chewie and Wrigley sipped hot chocolate in miniature mugs on a miniature bench nearby.

I was confident in my display. I was not, however, confident in my promotion of the Pawlidays Party itself. I had made some fliers and some social media invitations, but it wasn't reaching as many people as the first year's party had.

I called up the Chamber of Commerce and asked if we could schedule another meeting. I sat down in that same coffee shop with the Chamber's president and presented him my problem.

"The Happy Pawlidays Party is happening in less than two weeks, and I need help promoting it to *everyone* in the neighborhood."

Instantly, he was bursting with ideas. He made me a list of social media parent groups for our neighborhood and the adjacent ones. He took my fliers and said, "Send me a PDF of this flier. I'll run to our office and print out more of these."

When our meeting ended, he dashed to the Chamber's office, ran a bunch of prints of the flier, and went to a networking event that night for neighborhood teachers. He handed out the fliers to all the teachers there. Some of them even said, "Oh my goodness! That's Kringle on the flier! I recognize him! He's from ALIVE Rescue!"

Cliché as it may sound, it was a massive weight off my shoulders.

Running a business, especially when you're new at it, feels incredibly overwhelming to navigate by yourself. Well, the good news is, no one *has* to figure it out by themselves. That's why groups, societies, and clubs were created.

Here's my best advice to you: find some professional groups that cater to your specific geographical region or your industry. Not only will you meet some other fantastic business owners, you'll also find a group of people you can rely on, because they *get it*.

It was through a separate society that, in a roundabout way, I found my stuffed animal manufacturer. I joined the Society of Children's Book Writers and Illustrators (often abbreviated to SCBWI) in Chicago. I didn't think this organization would be able to help me much with the toy component of my business -- but I was wrong.

After attending writer networking events for about three years with SCBWI (where I always left my business card), I got a call from a number I didn't recognize. It was a woman who was at a networking event for SCBWI — one I wasn't even able to attend — who had gotten my business card from a different member.

"I have a plushie business, and I want to write a book," she explained. "Someone told me that you have a business that does both books and stuffed animals, so I was hoping you could give me some advice on the book part."

It just so happened that I had exactly the opposite of what she had: a business that needed to add stuffed animals. (At the time, we had just marked our handmade plushies "sold out" and were looking for a manufacturer. More on this story in Chapter 14.)

This woman was looking to get her books published in a different way than I did—she wanted to use a literary agent—so I gave her the emails of some friends I had who had agents representing them for their picture books. She gave me the email address and phone number of her stuffed animal manufacturer: a company called Adorable World.

Adorable World was exactly what I was looking for: small quantity production with reasonable per-unit prices. One of the biggest challenges to getting plushies manufactured (or getting *anything* manufactured) is that most companies want to produce items in high quantities—often in the tens of thousands. Well, I certainly didn't have the money to get 10,000 of each plushie (or 40,000 total plushies!) made at once. I could, however, work with a small-quantity manufacturer like Adorable World, whose minimums were 250 per design.

Because this other author and I belonged to the same writer's society, we were put into contact with one another when we both had information that could benefit the other. So, join a group or society that fits in with your mission or industry, meet as many people there as you can, and hand out business cards like they're free candy!

(Quick side note: Some organizations charge high prices for membership. Whether you want to pay to join a society will be a cost and benefit analysis you'll have to run based on your own personal circumstances. If connections are what you need *most* to grow, then a $100 membership fee for the year might be worth it! But also, keep in mind that many societies have financial aid or scholarships you can apply for on the website. I stopped paying for my membership to SCBWI back in 2016 because I was able to get my membership covered by speaking on one local author panel per year and forgoing a speaking fee. See if there are options like this available for you!)

Prioritize FRIENDSHIP!

yes!! b

The reason I consider networking a hobby sometimes, even though it's *technically* a necessity for my career, is that I treat networking very similarly to the way I treat making friends. This mindset has helped me approach professional situations free of stress, maintain genuine connections with people, and — oh yeah — build some incredible new friendships.

In my experience, there are two main benefits to approaching networking the same way you'd approach friendship. First, you remove the pressure of the stakes that come with a "professional" situation. Second, you will foster strong connections based on more than just a transactional give-and-take.

So, how do I approach networking like I would a friendship? Well, it all starts with letting go of all the business advice I gave you earlier in this chapter. (Notice I said it *starts* with that—not that you should ignore it forever!) What I mean is, don't whip out your business card the second you find out that someone works in a similar industry as you. Don't start trying to make deals before you've even said hello. If you don't treat your friendships as quid-pro-quo, you shouldn't treat your networking that way, either. And if you *do* treat your friendships that way, then… maybe you should be reading a Grant Cardone book instead.

The first time I ever ordered business cards, I got so excited about having a professional-looking piece of glossy cardstock in my hand that I forgot to treat networking like a friendship. This was back in 2016, when I was 23 years old, one year out of college, and still new to the author world. When I was at a YA authors' festival at a local bookstore in Chicago, I decided that I needed to network with every author, publisher, and editor there. Every time

I met a publisher or a bookstore owner, I would whip out my card, tell them about my books and my editing services, and shake their hand. I'm not sure if that came off as weird to them; looking back, it probably did, but I've struggled with my own self-awareness for a long time, so it didn't feel awkward to me. But let me tell you, in retrospect, *yes* that was awkward. And I'm 100 percent positive of it now, four years later, because I never heard from any of those people ever again.

Another time, also in 2016 (that was a rough year, for many reasons), I made a similar mistake. I went to a conference for CWIP, or Chicago Women in Publishing. At that conference, I heard that there would be publishers and university presses there. I decided to do what every young professional does before going to a networking event: print out copies of my resume. I used the printer in my apartment building's lobby to print multiple hard copies of my resume to bring along with me in a black folder. Every time I stopped at a table that looked interesting, I'd hand the person behind the table my resume and business card and let them know that I was interested if they were ever hiring.

Do you think I ever got a job, let alone made a lasting industry connection from this? The answer is a big, hard NO.

I never put in the time to foster a real connection with those people. Unlike my story of meeting a woman in the stuffed animal business through SCBWI, in these cases, I just marched up to people and made our first interaction a business transaction. I didn't think about how we could benefit one another, and I didn't think about building a connection beyond what I needed in the moment. That was not a way to start a strong connection or build a network.

By contrast, when I met Jan, I didn't approach her by shoving my business card in her face. I approached meeting her the way I would greet a new friend: I got excited that I was about to meet a new person who shared my love of writing, art, and creating children's books. Even though Jan is more than 40 years older than I am, at the time, I didn't think, "Wow, she's very connected, I need to leverage this ASAP!" Instead, I approached her table and saw a very sweet, happy lady behind it signing books filled with beautiful art. And I approached her with this mindset: We share a passion. Therefore, we can connect on an emotional level.

Look for Contacts Everywhere!

I met the illustrator of "Smile, Chewie!" on an airplane. It's one of my favorite stories to tell. Often, fellow authors who read Chewie's book ask me, "How did you find your illustrator?", often looking for ways to connect with an illustrator themselves.

I love when I get to answer, "On an airplane," because it always leads to a great story.

I was flying out to Philly to visit my grandma for her birthday back at the end of 2016. My family was scattered across two rows of airplane seats, and we were talking about some project I was writing. At the time, Furever Home Friends was not a business yet; I just had a rough draft of Princess Allee and a rough concept for *Smile, Chewie!* — not even an outline yet!

As we talked about something I was writing, a girl from across the aisle piped in, "Oh, are you an author?"

I was very new to being an author at this point, but you all know I've never been hurting for overconfidence, so I proudly said, "Yes!"

"Cool! I'm an illustrator!" she said. She explained that she was flying to Philly to return to her art school program after winter break ended.

I was instantly excited. I've never been a huge believer in fate, but this felt like one of the moments you just don't pass up. "We should team up some time!" I said. (I hadn't yet learned the word "collab.")

We traded business cards. She gave me her Instagram handle. Once the plane landed and I got cell phone service back, I followed her on social media. On the drive from the airport to the hotel, I started scrolling through her feed, and I noticed something: she was incredible at drawing animals and bringing them to life through watercolor paints.

When I returned home to Chicago, I started seeking out illustrators for the first two books in the Furever Home Friends series. One of the first people I reached out to was Christy, the girl from the plane. I asked her for sample work and for a quote on how much she'd charge per image if I hired her to do a 24-page, 12-spread picture book.

After I weighed the quality of her art along with her prices, she turned out to be the perfect match to illustrate Chewie's book. The friendly faces she created on her animals brought the exact vibe I was looking for with Furever Home Friends, and the joyful, whimsical use of watercolors gave the pictures a fun and childlike, yet still realistic and professional look that matched perfectly with our aesthetic. I was so excited to offer her a contract.

Whenever people ask me how I met the illustrator for *Smile, Chewie!*, where I found someone who could do such gorgeous art, I love telling the story of randomly meeting her on a plane.

Remember earlier, when I said I don't really believe in fate? I still don't. I don't really think that this encounter was fate or happenstance. It was a conscious effort on both of our parts to seek new opportunities everywhere we went.

I talk about being a writer *a lot*. Originally, I formed that habit because I like talking about writing—it's fun! And I just love to talk. But over time, I found that talking about writing had a benefit: the more you talk about something, the higher probability you'll end up talking to someone who can help you out. I didn't talk about my life as a writer *just* while I was on that plane; I talked about my life as a writer everywhere, *including* on the plane, and that was the one memorable event that came of it.

Christy was also open to opportunities. When she overheard a random person in an airplane seat nearby talking about writing books, she didn't have to pipe up with, "I'm an illustrator!" She could've done what we often do, what often feels natural: to just think, "Hmm, that's cool," in her head and then go back to whatever else she was doing. Instead, *she* sought opportunities everywhere as well. In the end, both of our open-mindedness helped her land an illustration job and it helped me find the Furever Home Friends' first employee.

As you start your business, I encourage you to seek opportunities everywhere you can. Talk about what you're doing to everyone who will listen. (Within reason; if your friends are like, "Hey, I want to talk about something other than your difficult decision between crowdfunding, loans, credit, and venture capital," then maybe you're taking it too far.)

Be proud of the work that you do and shout it from the rooftops. The person who needs your message most might just be there to hear it.

Say YES to New Opportunities!

Remember how, at the beginning of the chapter, I mentioned that my first major networking experience came from a mentorship program in my college marching band? Well, imagine my shock when almost *no one* I mentioned this program to had *any idea* what I was talking about. When I'd ask my other marching band friends who their mentors were, or if they liked that program, or if they even *remembered* that program, almost *all of them said they had no idea what this program was*. I think the program might've dissolved a year or two after I participated in it. Looking back, I feel ridiculously lucky that I'm one of the few people who participated.

Why didn't most people know what this program was? I can't say for sure. I'm not inside other people's heads. But if I had to guess, I'd say that most people probably overlooked the email, or forgot to schedule a call with their mentor, or talked to their mentor once or twice and then forgot about them. And honestly, those are totally reasonable things to do; senior year of college is *stressful*. If your senior year was anything like mine, then the career center was all up your butt about how your resume sucks, internships were chomping at the bit to hire you without pay, and you were getting a flood of emails from thinly-disguised pyramid schemes trying to recruit you based on that grossly outdated resume you put up on CareerBuilder. It would be so easy for one email about a mentorship program to fly under the radar.

I'm grateful that I remembered to click on that email. I'm grateful that I said YES to the opportunity to meet someone new, to learn from their experiences, and to *network*. I guess I don't know what else may have come from emails *I* unintentionally deleted or forgot to reply to. But based on how great this opportunity turned out for me, I would recommend that everyone say YES when a new opportunity like this comes along.

Your college alumni association is having a networking event specific to the field you want to enter? Say YES. A convention is coming to your city, and you know there will be people there who have created successful businesses you admire? Say YES. Your acquaintance from high school messages you on Facebook asking if you want to make a six-figure income from home by selling essential oil enemas? Say *hell no.* Your mom made friends at Costco with someone who makes the same kind of products you want to make? SAY YES.

Say yes to networking. (Say no to network marketing.) Say yes to making new friends. Say yes to making networking your new hobby. I love networking *so much*, that I'll even network with all of you right now. My email's in the introductory chapter. If I'm involved in a similar field as you, and you think we'd be mutually valuable connections, email me. Let's be friends!

12

Public Speaking is Fun!
I Promise!

If you haven't already noticed how big of a dork I am from reading this book, let me remove all doubt: I was a hardcore debate-team kid from 2004-2012. I did debate, speech team, and competitive public speaking for nearly a *decade*. That's right; competitive public speaking. In the previous chapter, I just talked about how networking is my only hobby, but I guess you could make a strong case for public speaking being a hobby too, just because of how much I *love* it.

Imagine my shock when high-school Savy, who loved nothing more than being the center of attention and had a trophy case full of *competitive public-speaking awards*, learned that public speaking is the number-one thing people list as their greatest fear, with the second-most common fear being *death*.

I was like, *Hold up. People are AFRAID of this shit? Why? It's so fun! I get to TALK competitively. I can win awards for being a straight-up blabbermouth! A talk-a-holic!* But then I grew a few years older, my brain matured, and I learned about this weird thing called *empathy*, where I can actually imagine how other people feel, and I realized that not everyone loves public speaking the way I do.

Public speaking is scary for a lot of people. I took some time to learn about *why* people are afraid of it. That included some online research on the Mayo Clinic, and a survey I sent out to about eighty co-workers a few years ago, asking them to list what it was about public speaking that made them nervous. Now that I've learned about all of that, it's time for me to share *my* perspective with you: why I *love* public speaking, and why I think you can learn to love it too. I will also share some of my best tips for public speaking in different circumstances. Enjoy!

Why Do I Need Public Speaking Skills as a Business Owner?

There are countless situations where public speaking skills will come in handy, but without having some concrete situations to visualize, sometimes it can be difficult to see the value in developing this skill.

In my process of running the Furever Home Friends, here are some instances where my comfort with public speaking has made everything easier:

- When a school hires Furever Home Friends to do an author visit, I love giving presentations to large groups of kids about the importance of reading and writing.
- I also do readings of my books to these groups of kids. Having an animated presence helps the kids engage with the stories.
- At book signings, I've done readings of my books to groups of adults, including animal shelter volunteers. Launch parties tend to include lots of readings!

But Savy, you might say, *my business has nothing to do with books! I will never have to do a school visit or a reading. Why should I care about public speaking?* Well, here are some other places that I've had to use public speaking, completely irrelevant of the fact that I sell books.

When I've entered pitch competitions, I've had to create short, focused speeches within 3-5-minute time constraints and present them to audiences of hundreds of people, including judge panels and potential investors. In 2018, I earned $2,600 in total grant money from pitch competitions.

- I've created and narrated short videos to advertise my business, which I put up on my YouTube channel. Because I'm comfortable with my ability as a speaker, I've saved money not having to hire another speaker or narrator.

- I speak to customers and other business owners one-on-one at festivals, conventions, and expos. When I have a booth at a large event, I always need to gain the attention of potential customers who are overwhelmed with the show floor's offerings.

Regardless of the field you're entering, having a strong, confident presence when addressing others, from large crowds, to small panels of investors, to individual customers, will only help you stand out.

Why is Public Speaking Fun?

Because you have the opportunity to share your message, uninterrupted.

Think about that for a second—it seems obvious, but in today's technology-dominated world, this opportunity is growing more and more rare. Audiences are bombarded with hundreds of images online every minute. Even when we see people in person, everyone has their cell phone with them. Now, I'm not saying that any of this is a bad thing. In fact, I think growth in technology and the influence of the internet has been a huge asset to most small business owners. I'll go into that even deeper in my chapter about Narrowcasting. However, opportunities for a captive audience with face-to-face interaction are rare. Which means that when you as a business owner should look forward to every single opportunity that comes your way.

The more we look at public speaking as an opportunity rather than an obstacle, the more we can learn to look forward to it. I look at every presentation, every sales pitch, and every reading as a chance to show others just how excited I am about this business. I view it as a vessel for my overflowing passion for this business. I look forward to every chance I get to tell people about my business and its mission, face to face, out loud.

Why Is Public Speaking Sometimes Scary?

According to the Mayo Clinic, stage fright is actually a form of anxiety. Our body responds with the same signals that cause anxiety in dangerous situations, because being in front of a crowd is something we *perceive* as dangerous. Many people often worry that they'll phrase something wrong, or that someone will notice you're not as knowledgeable on the topic as you thought you were, or that the whole world will expose you as a fraud.

I guess, from an evolutionary perspective, being the center of attention in a crowd *does* inspire fear. Think about it: when in the early days of human civilization did people stand before a big crowd? Well, if they were a world leader about to declare war, maybe. Or maybe they were a criminal about to be publicly executed. Regardless, public speaking is often associated with *big events* that have *big consequences*. But it doesn't have to be!

My best recommendation for overcoming performance anxiety is some good old-fashioned journaling. If you have a big business pitch coming up, or a big presentation you have to make, or a big livestream you're about to give to all your YouTube followers as you release your new book, take a few minutes beforehand to examine your emotions. How are you feeling about it? Do you feel nervous? Where in your body do you hold that nervousness? Does your chest feel fluttery? Does your head pound? Do your shoulders feel tense? Write these things down.

Then, start journaling about what your fears *actually are*. Force yourself to look deep into what is causing you to feel nervous. And then, for each of those *specific* fears, write two things: 1) how likely it is to happen, and 2) a solution.

Here's an example:

I'm afraid to give this pitch because the whole audience is going to laugh at me and think I'm really stupid.

Okay. How likely is this to happen? Not very likely, if you ask me. Take a moment to visualize the audience: are you speaking to an audience full of literal toddlers? (Hey, I sometimes do! Children's author, remember?) In that case, recontextualize your feelings on them laughing at you—making kids laugh is a *good* thing! And if you're talking to adults? Well, the truth is, most adults have learned some degree of social etiquette and know not to laugh at a presenter. You can conclude that this fear is irrational. You can cross it off your list and move onto the next one!

Let's try another one:

I'm afraid to give this pitch because I'm worried I'll forget to explain some of my most important points about the business.

Okay. How likely are you to forget something when you're nervous in front of a crowd? Fairly likely. So, this is a rational fear.

What's a solution to this fear? *I can write down some major points on a notecard that I can reference in my hand while I give my pitch. Or I can put the most important points on a slideshow so I can see them as I present, and then I won't forget. I can send an email to the person in charge of the event right now to find out if I can have a hookup for a slideshow or PowerPoint. I can also practice running through my pitch a few times to make sure I've gotten those parts nailed down.*

See? Now you have a concrete plan of action for overcoming this fear. Let's try one more.

I'm afraid to give this talk about my business because I'm worried someone will ask me a question I don't know the answer to.

How likely is that to happen? *Not that likely, since I'm the most knowledgeable person about this topic in the room. Still, it's completely possible that it could happen!*

Okay. Since you're the most knowledgeable person in the room, your first step is to take a moment and reflect on that. *You* know the most on this out of everyone here. Internalize that truth and own it! But, like you mentioned, you *could* still land in the clutches of the infamous "gotcha" question. Time to dig a little deeper.

What types of questions do you think your audience might ask you? *I don't know. I can't read people's minds.*

Okay, fair enough. In that case, your solution might be to look at the attendance for the event where you'll be speaking. See if you can do any background research on your audience members and what knowledge they're likely to have. Then, come up with a plan for what to do if you get a question you don't know how to answer. Maybe have a phrase ready to go, like, "That's a great question! You know, I'll have to research that further; let me know if you want to talk one-on-one after the presentation." Then, practice saying that phrase to the mirror.

Once again, you have a plan of action to combat that fear.

Best Tips for Public Speaking

We've covered the positive aspects of public speaking and we've also addressed why it can sometimes feel like a difficult hurdle to overcome. We've talked about strategies to overcome fear and put your best, most confident self forward. But... now what?

You're ready to give a speech or a presentation! The only thing left to figure out is... what exactly am I going to say and how am I going to say it?

Know Your Audience

When you're speaking to any group of people, you need to know what *that specific group* is looking for. Think of it this way: as a business owner, you already know about identifying your target customer. In a way, your audience is its own form of target customer; you have to figure out how to meet *their* needs.

The demographics of your audience should influence your approach to public speaking. For example, on my YouTube channel, my target audience is other authors, fans of YA literature in their 20s-30s, and adults interested in learning about the business side of writing. Hear that? *Adults*. If you're been to my YouTube channel, you've probably heard me drop more than a few f-bombs. You've also probably seen me have a beer live on camera while talking about a controversial topic, like business guru scammers.

Now, could you imagine in I walked into a room of kindergartners for a Furever Home Friends book reading, shotgunned a beer real quick, and shouted, "Fuck that traffic this morning, am I right?" I would never be allowed in a school again!

That's an extreme example, but regardless of how nuanced your situation may be, figuring out the needs of your audience is the first step to a successful public speaking experience.

<u>When figuring out how to appeal to your audience, you might ask yourself these questions:</u>

- What age is the majority of my audience? Is there a minimum age?
- If my audience falls into a particular age group, are there certain cultural references that they're more likely to understand?
- If my audience is from a different generation than I am, will there be any background information I have to give them?
- What expectations do my audience have for this event? Are they planning to be entertained by a funny book reading? Are they hoping to learn something from an informative business pitch?

We've all seen that person at a party (or, in today's socially distanced age, on Twitter) who doesn't know how to "read the room." None of us want to *be* that person. The first step to properly reading the (literal) room is to determine *who* is in that room in the first place.

To Script or Not to Script?

There are times when I just walk into a room and speak off the cuff; there are *other* times when I have scheduled *every single word* I say ahead of time. Some people worry that scripting out an entire speech or presentation will make you sound like a robot—and that could very well happen. Conversely, some people worry that if you *don't* script out your presentation, you'll end up floundering your way through every sentence and forgetting your main points.

So, to script or not to script? That is the question! (That wasn't plagiarism. Shakespeare's public domain, y'all.) And the answer, much like everything else in business, is circumstantial. It all comes down to knowing your audience and knowing your situation.

For example, one speech I *absolutely* scripted was my pitch at the 2018 Purpose Pitch competition. At this event, four finalists had five minutes to pitch their businesses to a group of experts for a chance to win grant money as well as the title of "Most Purposeful Startup in Chicago." Five minutes was the absolute time limit. If you spoke longer than five minutes, a moderator would cut you off, and then you'd risk leaving out important information about your business. So, it was important that I planned out *every single thing* I wanted to say and practiced it ahead of time.

For this speech, I wrote and re-wrote my script multiple times. There was money on the line — *thousands of dollars!* For me, as a brand-new business owner at the time, that money could make a huge difference for the future growth of my company. I needed to make sure that each judge knew exactly why my business had potential and exactly why we needed the money to achieve those goals.

By contrast, when I'm talking at a launch party, I'll talk completely off the cuff. If I'm presenting my newest book to an audience at the launch party, or I'm getting ready to talk about my process of writing it and then take a Q&A from the audience, it's important for me to be conversational and friendly; I'm not here to talk *at* you, I'm here to talk *with* you. Because of that, I don't script my speeches for these events. That way, I stay out of the mindset of creating a presentation, and instead view the audience as friends.

There's also a middle ground between full-on scripting and completely impromptu talking. That middle ground is where my school visits live. When I visit a school to talk to kids about the reading and writing process, I will often have an outline of talking points rather than a full-on script. That way,

I make sure that I cover everything that the teacher is expecting, but I also can tailor my approach to that group and what questions they have.

This also comes back to knowing your audience. For example, when I speak to a group of sixth graders, I'll have a PowerPoint presentation with discussion topics about my journey as an author, my best advice for the writing process, etc. If I'm talking to a group of preschoolers, I'll focus more on the content of the books themselves. I'll read each book out loud to the kids, and then we'll talk through the discussion questions at the end together. It would be weird to read a picture book to a group of sixth graders who likely already enjoy reading novels. It would also be weird to talk to preschoolers about determining their purpose when approaching a piece of writing.

Keeping my school visit preparations loose and malleable has helped me adapt it to each audience.

Have Fun with Tongue Twisters!

Tongue twisters can be silly, but they're also really helpful for practicing consonant and vowel articulation. If you tend to slur your words, regular practice of tongue twisters can help you out.

When saying a tongue twister, start out saying it *slowly*. Make sure you feel *each* vowel and consonant in your mouth. How does your tongue move when you say each letter? Is your throat more or less open on certain vowels compared to others? Do your teeth close when emphasizing a certain consonant? When do you close your lips?

Once you know *exactly* how to move your mouth to say each syllable clearly, start picking up speed on that tongue twister.

For me, the oral articulation I developed from this process evolved into my "public speaking voice." Don't get me wrong; you want to use *your* voice—your *real* voice, not a deeper or fancier sounding voice, and *absolutely* not any accents!—but you want to use the clearest version of your voice.

After I practiced tongue twisters for a while, I was eventually able to switch that version of my voice on and off. It starts to feel natural.

My suggestion is to Google a few tongue twisters that really challenge your speaking voice. Work on these. Then, when you're approaching a big event in front of a crowd, say a few of them to yourself ahead of time to get warmed up!

Pacing is Everything!

Have you ever seen someone get nervous during a presentation, start wishing for the sweet release of death, and speed-talk their way through their points just to get it over with faster? I think we've all probably seen something like that at one point or another, and likely, many of us have *done* that as well. Talking super fast defeats the purpose of even giving your presentation in the first place, since the audience likely won't be able to hear all of your points or retain them. On the flip side, sometimes we see someone talking slowly, taking pauses as they try to figure out what to say next, and bringing the energy in the room down to nap-time levels. That's not a good way to keep your audience's attention, either.

Just like in a book or a movie, the pacing of a speech or presentation can make or break it. You'll want to hit that sweet spot between speed-talking and plodding your way through. Often, this means talking much slower than you would in everyday conversation, since you want to give your audience time to process everything you're saying. However, when trying to talk slower than usual, it's easy to *overcompensate* and end up talking at the speed of molasses.

When I'm practicing the pacing for a presentation, a basic rule of thumb I use is to talk at a speed of 150-180 words per minute. This is just a starting point, of course. There will be times that you want to speed up to indicate something exciting is happening or slow down to emphasize the importance of a certain point.

If you're new to pacing yourself when you talk, I suggest starting small. Go online, find a passage from an article, and copy and paste about 180 words of it into a document. Then, set a stopwatch on your phone. (Or on an actual stopwatch. We used those back when I was on the debate team. I had a flip phone with an antenna back then. Am I old yet?)

Time yourself. See how long it takes you to get through reading it aloud in your normal talking voice. Did it take you way longer than a minute? Did it take you only 30 seconds? Try adjusting your talking pace to get as close to one minute as possible.

Another suggestion is to record yourself. (Back when I was learning public speaking, I had to do this with a camcorder that only took full VHS tapes. *Am I old yet?!?!*) Pull out your phone and record a video of yourself saying those words. Then, play it back. How well can you understand yourself?

Finding the right pace doesn't happen instantly. But through consistent practice and repetition, a good pace will become second nature. And that leads me to my final tip.

Practice Practice Practice!

Remember when I said I once had five minutes to pitch my business to a group of judges to win grant money? And I said that of course, I scripted *the entire thing*, because it was important to make sure I got every point in there? Yeah, I practiced that about a million times.

I practiced it for my mom. I practiced it for Tyler. I practiced it for Chewie. I practiced it for the mirror in the school bathroom. (I was barely ever home in 2018.)

Like any skill, public speaking gets better with practice! Block out some time in your schedule for practicing if you have an event coming up. That way, you'll get the chance to practice timing yourself, getting the pace right, articulating all the right consonants, and emphasizing all the right words. All of these skills come together through *practice*.

Now, go speak to someone publicly! But not that publicly. Maybe do it over Zoom. (As I mentioned before, I started writing this book back when "pandemic" was a collaborative strategy-based board game. But anyway.) Go present your ideas to the world!

yep's

13

The Big Moment: Making a Sale!

Fun fact: I used to think I *hated* sales. Nothing scared me more than asking someone straight up if they wanted to hand me their money. I blame this fear entirely on my past working in telemarketing; the second I asked for the sale was the second the annoyed person on the other end of the phone was sure to hurl a variety of R-rated insults at me. This anxiety stayed with me like a Pavlovian response long after I'd quit my very last job with *high-volume sales* in the description.

It's been almost five years since I last worked in a job that could be categorized as corporate sales, call-center work, or cold calling. Over those past five years, I discovered something: I *don't* hate sales. As it turns out, making a sale gives me a caffeinated

189

rush. It excites me. It indicates to me that someone *wants* what I've created.

Of course, not *everyone* is going to want what I've created. Believe it or not, there are people out there who *don't* want cute books or plushies about dogs! I know, I was shocked, too. But in the past two years of running this business, I've learned to overcome that fear of rejection and craft a sales pitch that I can use over and over again.

In this chapter, I'll break down the different elements of how I make a sale. Keep in mind that what it means to make a sale is going to be different for every industry. Also, because I'm going to cover online sales, social media marketing, and building a platform on the internet in Part 3, I'm going to focus primarily on making sales face-to-face in this chapter, in addition to going over the basics of how sales works.

Some companies, like mine, are B2C: business-to-consumer. That means we produce goods or services to be purchased directly by the customer. Most businesses that sell a product through a store or online retailer are B2C. If you're planning to create a product that you want someone to consume—like starting a bakery, designing your own clothing brand, or producing music—your business is B2C as well.

The opposite of this would be a B2B company: business-to-business. These companies produce goods or services that are intended for other businesses to use, but not the end customer. For example, a factory that produces car parts would likely be a B2B company; they aren't intending to sell car parts to random people on the street, but to car companies or mechanic shops. Similarly, a company that sells online ad space would be B2B as well. These companies want other businesses to buy ad space so that the *other* company can reach their customers.

Some companies are a combination of both B2B and B2C. For example, you might want to start a graphic design service. Your service could design logos for businesses, but might also do custom work for individual people who need personal signs or banners made.

It's not crucial that your company fits perfectly into the B2B or B2C box, but it is important that you know how these distinctions will affect your approach to sales. If you're primarily a B2C business, your goal is going to be finding *customers* who want to buy products directly from you. However, if you're a B2B business, you'll be looking to find *clients* and *partners*. Because my company, Furever Home Friends, is a B2C business, that's the framework I'll be using in this chapter to break down my process of creating a sales pitch and reaching customers. However, I hope if you are running a B2B company, that you can still apply some of these principles to your business as well.

Approaching Potential Customers

Approaching customers can mean different things in different contexts. In my business, I approach customers in a few different ways based on where I am. The first step in approaching your customers is to figure out *where* you can find them.

For me, that's often at events where people are looking to shop. I like to set up a booth at local street festivals, craft fairs, literary festivals, small business expos, and comic or entertainment conventions. However, I've also found other places where my potential customers might be patronizing. Because my focus is on dogs, I once hosted a book signing in the pet department of a larger home goods store in the Chicago suburbs. I've hosted many book signings at smaller, independently owned pet stores, since that's where the dog people are going to be. I've also set up tables at local artisan markets, local bookstores, and more.

When determining new places that I can find my potential customers, here are some questions I might ask myself:

- Who is my target customer? (Dog lovers, parents, teachers, toy aficionados, etc.)

Where does my target customer like to shop? (Pet stores, toy stores, bookstores, local Chicago markets, etc.)

 Where might many of my target customers be at once, specifically looking to spend money? (A local author night at a bookstore, a pet expo, a convention, a craft fair, etc.)

 How can I get myself in front of those customers? (Find the names of the owners of local pet stores. Find their email addresses and reach out to schedule a time to come in and sell books/plushies. Research the names of purchasing managers at local bookstores. Find the contact information for the companies who put on local conventions and craft fairs. Google is my friend here!)

Once you've determined *where* your customers are, it's time to figure out how to grab their attention.

During my first few events, grabbing customers' attention was one of the hardest puzzles to solve. Sure, at my own book launch parties and book signings, I had people there *for* the Furever Home Friends; but what about the events where no one had heard of me? What about local festivals and craft fairs, where I was hoping to discover *new* customers?

When there are tons of artists and vendors all around you competing for the same audience's attention, sometimes it can feel difficult to break through the noise. Even I, as a constantly attention-seeking extrovert, found it a little awkward to just shout, "Hey! Come over here! Look at what I'm selling!" to random people I'd never met.

That's why I developed a tight, attention-seeking pitch that I can quickly shout at all passersby at every event. Now, calling it a "pitch" feels a little gross. While, yes, my end goal is *always* to make a sale, I don't like looking at this process as a transaction. When getting to know a potential new customer, I like to think of it as a path to making a new connection. I could meet a new dog person! I could hear someone's story of how they rescued their pet! There are so many things I could do other than just make a sale—even if that *is* my goal. So maybe it would be better to call this interaction an *icebreaker* rather than a pitch.

Here's how my icebreaker goes:

Wait until someone passes by my table. Are they within 3 feet of my table in any given direction? Have they made eye contact with me or with any of my products? Are they looking at my booth? Okay, let's go!

"Hey, we've got some books and plushies based on real rescue dogs and their stories of getting adopted! If you're a dog person, come check it out!"

Generally, in this moment, people will either nod and walk away, or they'll go, "Oh my goodness, that's so cute!" and come up to my table to talk to me further. That's when we move into the next step.

The "Ask"

In sales, there's a moment called "the ask." That's the moment when you straight-up ask the other person if they want to buy what you're selling. This, for me, was one of the most difficult moments to execute properly, because at its core it's hard selling, but you're trying to make it seem like it *isn't* hard selling.

My days working as a telemarketer had jaded me against the ask; when I would ask someone over the phone if they'd like to invest in some online advertising, I was usually met with an annoyed person on the other end either getting ready to yell at me or hang up. That's why I had to reframe my thinking surrounding "the ask."

One of my favorite events to attend every year is the Printers Row Lit Fest in Chicago. It's a summer book festival that features authors from around the country speaking on panels along with dozens of tents filled with local Chicago authors, publishers, and booksellers. Every year, I meet tons of awesome customers at this event and add some new dog people to the Furever Home Friends family.

During the 2018 Printers Row Lit Fest, I was sharing a table with a fellow children's book author. While I was doing okay with my sales, I noticed that his were booming. Part way through the day, he turned to me and said, "Why aren't you asking people if they want to buy?"

He explained that at the end of his interaction with every customer, he'd say something along the lines of, "So, are you interested in buying one?" While the majority of people would answer with something like, "I'm not sure," or "Maybe I'll come back later" (which sounds like a lie, but you'd be shocked at how many people actually *do* come back to buy later after making a full circuit around the festival), many people would also answer with, "Yeah, you know what, I think I'd like to buy one!" Either way, it was necessary to put the idea of *making a purchasing decision* into the customer's head. Then, in that moment, they could decide. Otherwise, the interaction could just go on aimlessly forever.

My initial response was, "I don't know if I can just *ask someone to buy something*. That's kind of awkward."

His response? "Who cares if it's awkward?"

I reflected on that for a moment; he was right. Why *was* I worried about a potentially awkward interaction? At an event with hundreds of other authors and thousands of readers, why does it matter if a few interactions are awkward?

I took his advice and started doing "the ask." At the end of the weekend, I took inventory and realized that I had sold the *most books* of *any* event I'd done so far. It was like Black Friday came in the middle of June for me.

Over the years, I've refined and reworked my "ask." Here are some examples of asks I've used:

- "If you're interested in getting one of the books, I can sign it and address it to whoever you're planning to give it to—even if it's your dog!"
- *Sees customer reading* Princess Allee *and flipping through the pages.* "Were you interested in getting *Princess Allee* today?"
- To level up, I've even tried upselling. *Sees customer reading* Princess Allee *and flipping through the pages.* "Are you interested in getting Allee's plushie as well, or just the book?"

The "ask" does not always result in a sale. I judge my success by seeing if 1% of the people at an event buy; I expect to interact with 10% of total guests at a festival (though I always aim for more; the goal should always be to interact with *every* guest at an event, even if that's physically impossible), and out

This!

of that 10%, I hope that 10% will buy from me. This was a rule I used when I started running my first Kickstarter. Someone told me that statistically, 1% of people who see the average Kickstarter campaign will contribute. Which meant that if I wanted to get 100 contributors, I needed to make sure that at least 10,000 people saw the campaign.

The same is true at events. If I'm hoping that at least 10% of people who stop at my table will buy from me, the best way to increase my sales is by interacting with more people. Like I mentioned in the previous paragraph, my goal is always to interact with *everybody*. At a large convention with 200,000 people in attendance, that's probably impossible. But sometimes I like setting impossible goals, even with the knowledge that I'll fall short, because it forces me to reach higher than I thought I could.

Of course, the ask comes with an obvious risk. If you're interacting with hundreds of people and giving them all "the ask," and statistically, most people will say no… how do you handle that?

The Fear of Rejection

My fear of rejection was *strong* when I started selling to customers one-on-one. With my background in telemarketing, I wasn't surprised I had that fear. Before I worked in telemarketing, I had no fear of rejection whatsoever. If I wanted something, I asked for it, applied for it, or found out how to get it. But once you spend eight hours a day getting screamed at on the phone (and for a good reason, since you disrupted someone's day to call them about something they have no interest in; don't work in telemarketing if you can help it), that fear starts to grow in your stomach, getting bigger and bigger until it's a giant monster, and all you can hope is that it won't break through your skin like in the movie *Alien*.

The good news is that no Fear Monster has ever actually leapt out of my stomach and destroyed my insides. Which means it probably won't happen for you, either. Also, when you're talking to people that already came to an event that you're at, you're not calling a stranger in the middle of the day and disrupting them, so the chances of someone screaming at you are very, very low. In fact, while I've had many *very, very strange* interactions with customers (which I'll detail in the final chapter of this book), no one has ever yelled at me for talking to them. I've talked to thousands of people one-on-one over the past two years of doing frequent events, and — let me repeat that — *no one* has *ever* yelled at me for talking to them.

My approach to sales is different than a lot of other successful businesspeople, so feel free to take my advice here with a grain of salt. But one of the reasons I stopped working in telemarketing was the way we were told to respond to the word "no"; in sales, we were told "no" is not a real answer. Ever heard the phrase, "Never take no for an answer?" Yeah, it makes me super uncomfortable too. During that time, I was taught that every time someone said, "No," it didn't mean "no," it meant, "I have an objection to this that you can solve through more prodding." That prodding led to very frustrated clients, which is a reason I started to fear rejection.

Now, I look at sales a lot like I look at the process of dating or making new friends: approach people with a genuine interest, and if they're not interested... well, I like to follow the very basic advice of, "No means no."

That means that there have been times when I've approached a potential customer with my usual pitch and they've responded with, "Well, I'm not really interested." In telemarketing, I was taught to respond to that by asking them what their hesitations were and then refuting those hesitations. However, now that I own my own business, I can choose to deem that a waste of time. If someone isn't interested in my product, I'll just say, "Awesome, have a good day," or, "That's fine, it was nice to meet you anyway!"

The only time I will try to *convince* someone to buy a product when they weren't planning to is if I have a legitimate suggestion. For example, I've had customers at my booth say things like, "I love these books and want to support this cause, but I don't have any kids in my life to buy them for." Then, I might jump in with a suggestion like, "Well, you could get it for your dog! I read to Chewie all the time." This does work occasionally; I've signed quite a few books to people's dogs. I've also made a few sales with a response like, "In that case, maybe you could get them to donate to a children's hospital or local school."

This strategy has helped me overcome my fear of rejection; the "no means no" premise has taken away pretty much all my anxiety about approaching new customers. As it turned out, it wasn't rejection I was afraid of; it was the requirement that I force a continued conversation with someone who was trying to push me away. This way, I have more time to talk in-depth with people who *do* show interest.

My best advice to you is to talk to *every single person* you meet when trying to sell face-to-face. If they aren't interested, move onto the next one. You'll likely have some interesting conversations and maybe even make some new friends.

14

To Scale or Not to Scale?

At the end of August 2017, my mom and I were drowning in a pile of flannel fabric and Poly-fil fluff. Our hands were about to fall off; hers even more than mine. She was spending hours every day cutting out the pieces for each stuffed animal from the custom pattern she'd created for each design, then sewing the bodies together, then handing them over to me — the other person on our small assembly line — to stuff their bodies, limbs, and tails tight with fluff.

After completing our first sixty-three orders — enough to fulfill all the preorders we received from the first Kickstarter — my mom said something I should've thought of months ago: "Hand-making all these stuffed animals was a terrible idea. After these are done, we are making no more of these."

It was a rough realization that two people couldn't produce that many stuffed animals to keep up with orders. Looking back, it seems painfully obvious; but deep down, I knew that we couldn't afford to get the plushies produced in bulk from a manufacturer, so without making them by hand, we wouldn't be able to sell them at all. Regardless, my mom was right; for the sake of avoiding tendonitis and carpal tunnel, we had to stop making them.

I marked the plushies as "sold out" on the website. It stung not being able to offer our precious plush friends; after all, the stuffed animal component was an important part of what made the Furever Home Friends more than a book series. The plushies all came with cute, customized adoption certificates. "Adopting" a stuffed animal was part of the Furever Home Friends experience.

I was stuck; how could I continue to sell these stuffed animals when we had no means to get any more of them produced? Obviously, getting them mass-produced by a professional stuffed animal company would be a necessity, which meant that my next step was to save up enough money to get a bulk order of each plush.

In other words, it meant it was time to *scale* my business.

What Does It Mean to Scale?

Scaling a business is the process of taking it to the next level. Basically, it's all the things you need to do for your business to grow, including buying more inventory, reaching more customers, attending bigger events or conferences, and maybe even hiring more employees. If you've ever watched *Shark Tank*, you've probably seen a lot of businesses trying to scale. Often, a business will go on that show to ask for an investment because they can't afford to take the business to the next level, but without taking the business to the next level, they'll never become profitable.

For example, in my business, I needed to start getting stuffed animals produced by a manufacturer, since handmaking them was no longer feasible. Manufacturers only produce items in bulk quantities. What was nice about handmaking the stuffed animals was that we could make one whenever an order came in; we didn't have to drop thousands of dollars on a bulk order. However, handmaking them was no longer sustainable.

When you scale a business, you make everything about it bigger: the production is bigger, the customer base is bigger, and, of course, the *money* required to run it is bigger.

Obstacles to Scaling

The biggest, most obvious obstacle to scaling a business is the same as the biggest, most obvious obstacle to *starting* a business: money. I couldn't afford to pay for a minimum bulk order of stuffed animals: that was a fact. Therefore, that became my biggest obstacle when scaling my business for the first time. As a result, my goal shifted to saving enough money and raising enough money to make that purchase.

Another obstacle you might face when trying to scale your business is time.

Finally, scaling your business might require bringing additional humans into the mix. I know, as business owners, we're all major workaholics who can't get enough of the grind, but at some point, the amount of work required *will* become too difficult for one person to handle. When you reach that point where you can no longer design all your own products, create them by hand, package them up, ship them, find new customers on social media, and create endless free content online to build your audience... maybe it's time to hire someone.

What's nice about hiring an employee is that you can find someone who's specialized in the fields where you're weakest. We all have our individual strengths and weaknesses. For me, writing is a strength. Public speaking is a strength. Online marketing is a weakness. That's why recently, I hired a social media manager to help me with the Furever Home Friends internet presence.

Startup Capital and Scaling

Earning the money to scale your business can be remarkably similar to the process of raising money to start it up. The techniques discussed in the "Starting with Startup Capital" section would work here as well.

When it came time for me to scale my business, I used the technique I discussed the most in that chapter: crowdfunding. In the spring of 2019, I ran my second Kickstarter campaign, this time to raise the funds necessary for my first bulk order of the stuffed animals. The manufacturer I was working with required a minimum order of 200 pieces per character, meaning I needed to have about $6,000 to pay them all at once. At that point, I was constantly putting every cent I earned back into the business (other than what I used to pay my own living expenses), so I did not have an extra $6,000 lying around. I barely had a couple hundred dollars as a safety net in my account. So, back to Kickstarter I went.

(If you remember in my first chapter, I mentioned that I had a weird stock market fixation as a kid. Part of that $6,000 I needed came from pulling my money out of the stock market. But that money wasn't enough to cover it, which is why I also ran a Kickstarter. Just thought I'd clarify that in case anyone's checking this book for continuity.)

What's nice about scaling a business rather than starting one is that you (hopefully) already have some customers. When I started my second Kickstarter campaign, I already had a newsletter full of the people who contributed to the first one, plus I had all the customers I'd met at festivals, book signings, and school visits.

Of course, crowdfunding isn't the only way to raise the funds to scale your business. There are infinite ways to raise the money. In some cases, you might want to take out a loan. In some cases, you might just want to save every bit of extra money you receive until you have enough for that big necessary purchase, whether that's a bulk order, a bigger space rental, or a new employee.

Is Scaling Always the Answer?

The short answer to this question is: No. The *long* answer to this question is: Nooooo. (Sorry, I just really wanted to make that dumb joke again.) The long answer is that, like everything in business, whether to scale is a complex decision with multiple factors to weigh.

Some businesses need to scale once and then they're set for life. Some businesses will need to keep scaling as they grow. Other businesses will *never* need to scale. Here are some examples.

If you want to start an Etsy shop as a side gig, but never plan to quit your full-time job, your business might never need to scale. If you have a small customer base and can keep up with handmaking objects for them, go for it!

If you want to start a neighborhood restaurant, your business might need to scale once as you grow your customer base and save money to buy cheaper ingredients in bulk. But that doesn't mean you need to turn your restaurant into a chain with multiple locations. You *can* if you want to, but it's not required; not all small businesses have to become big businesses. A small business can thrive as-is for life.

Let me repeat that:

Not all small businesses have to become big businesses.

Not! All! Small! Businesses! Have! To! Become! Big! Businesses!

I almost feel like I need the clap emoji for emphasis right now.

I think there's a stigma in the business world that we should always have growth as our number-one priority. While a growth mindset is good for keeping yourself motivated, there's no *requirement* that growth be your focus. If you want to run a small business, run a small business! Don't let anyone tell you that your business *needs* to expand if it doesn't.

If you're operating at a profit and all pieces of your business are running sustainably, just keep up the good work.

yes!

Part 4

The Scary World of Social Media

15

Why I Spelled My Name Wrong in the Title

Hi. I'm Savy, and I sold my soul for SEO.

I'll bet some of you were wondering this since you saw that the book's title and author name didn't match: if my name is Savy, and I'm a business owner, shouldn't I have titled the book *Savy Business Owner*?

Why did I call it *#SavvyBusinessOwner*, all one word, with a hashtag at the beginning, while putting an extra V in my first name? Why did I choose to *spell my own name wrong* in a book about my own business experiences?

For SEO.

For those of you new to SEO, it's an acronym that stands for search engine optimization. Basically, that means you're strategically choosing names for things, words to put in your social media posts, etc. based on what will show up first in the average user's online searches.

There's a joke that goes: "If you murder someone, where's the best place to hide the body? On the second page of Google search results, because no one looks there." (I found a variation of that joke on Elon Musk's Twitter. Citing my sources, y'all!)

The truth is, lots of people don't have the patience to look at multiple pages of results when searching for something online. That's why companies will *pay* sites like Google, YouTube, Facebook, Yelp, and others to put their business *first* for certain searches.

Google isn't the only search engine out there, even if it's the only one most people would name. Most social media sites act like search engines too. In fact, most of us already practice SEO on social media regularly; we use hashtags. Our hashtags help our posts show up in popular searches, which leads more people to our pages.

Okay, but *why* did I call my book *#SavvyBusinessOwner*? Because it's a popular hashtag on Instagram already. Am I copying Sophia Amoruso, founder of Nasty Gal, who wrote a business book called #*Girlboss*? Yeah, maybe. But I like my title better.

People are already searching and typing #SavvyBusinessOwner on Instagram every day. By choosing this title, I'm helping my book show up in more people's social media feeds, which will inform more people about the book's existence.

Plus, most people already spell my name wrong anyway, so I've just given up.

Now, I'm no expert on SEO. It's actually something I've been trying to learn more about as I grow my business. But what I've learned so far is, when a lot of people are actively searching for something, *jump on it.*

In 2017, when I was starting Furever Home Friends, I tried making a few YouTube videos about it. Since I love making and editing videos, and I watch YouTube way more often than actual TV or movies, I thought it would be a great next step for me. But in 2017, I had no idea how to make my videos searchable. As a result, I made a ton of vlogs about Chewie, unboxing videos showing off my book proofs, and book trailers advertising the business. Almost no one saw these. What was I doing wrong?

At one point, I thought I'd almost gotten the hang of SEO. When my new-adult LGBT novel *Sculpt Yourself* was coming out, I made a video about my own struggles with body image and how they related to the book. I titled this video "Having Huge Boobs Sucks." That video *killed it* in the search results. My channel had only about 40 subscribers, but this video was getting *thousands* of views. The problem was, it was clickbait. I looked at the video's analytics. As I'm sure you can assume, the audience was over 90% male. And the average view time was 23 seconds. Basically, guys were searching "huge boobs" on YouTube, finding my video, watching for a few seconds, realizing I was going to talk about a book and keep my shirt on the whole time, and closing the tab to head to PornHub, where they should've gone in the first place.

Getting the hang of SEO and searchability was a very slow, agonizing process. Half of it was tirelessly making content and the other half was screaming into an endless abyss where no one's listening. Which leads us into our next chapter!

16

Screaming into the Void

Here's what no one ever told me about starting my own business, but I *wish* someone had: the first few months feels like nonstop screaming into a void. If I'd known this, the process probably wouldn't have been any easier, but at least I'd have been mentally prepared.

What do I mean by *screaming into the void*? I mean that you're yelling over and over and over again, but no one's hearing you, or no one's responding.

The hard truth is, unless you're already famous, when you start a business, no one really cares. Sure, your family and friends are likely excited for you. They're probably happy to see you following your dreams. You've probably had a lot of people congratulate you, and you've probably gotten a few orders from people who already know who you are.

But the internet, which is inundated with nonstop information every second, and the public, which already has advertisements bombarding them everywhere they go from morning until night, does not care that another business has entered the game.

It sucks! You have this message that you really, *really* want everyone to hear! You have a great, revolutionary product that you genuinely believe is going to make everyone's lives better! You want to tell *everyone* about it! But no one's hearing you. You're telling people over and over — posting on social media, running advertisement campaigns, collaborating with other brands, etc. — but it all gets lost in a void.

It wasn't until I'd been running the Furever Home Friends for a full year that I started to get it: a business doesn't just gain momentum overnight. You don't find one magical way of marketing, or one magical technique, that suddenly turns your life around. Instead, you try a lot of things that don't work. Then, you find one that starts to work a little bit. You notice a *slight* increase in orders. Then you hit that technique harder, and then you notice a bigger increase, which is still small compared to where you want to be. And you do that over and over again, trying variations on that technique that will undoubtedly fail, until you find the one variation that just *slightly* works once again. And as a result, your business grows at the speed of molasses. But it *grows*.

For me, this tiny catalyst came in the form of YouTube. I'd always loved making videos, and I enjoyed making little ads, commercials, and videos about my Furever Home Friends products. I loved making little vlogs for Chewie so that customers could see my behind-the-scenes process. I posted these videos on YouTube, Facebook, Twitter, and Instagram. You know how many people saw them? Like eight or so. Almost no one; I was a nobody with no following.

Then, at the end of 2018, I found this community called BookTube. There was an entire group of people on YouTube who loved making videos just to talk about books! This was amazing! So, I started making videos with "BookTube" in the title, and people in this book community started finding me. I started commenting on their videos and getting involved in the community. We subscribed to each other's channels. Next thing I knew, I had 50 new subscribers pretty much overnight. Not a ton of new people, but for me, who had basically no audience before, it was *everything*. So, I decided to keep doing that. I started seeking out even *more* people, commenting on *more* videos, and finding *more* friends. And it worked. *Slowly.*

Every day, I'd notice a few more people had viewed my videos, or a few more people had commented, or a few more people had subscribed. And over time, I started to notice that every month, I was selling a few more books than I was the last month. When I'd go on YouTube and see videos of people reviewing my books or unboxing my plush dogs, it became crystal clear: building a YouTube audience was *very slowly* helping me grow my customer base.

I cannot stress enough how *slow* this was! We all love to hear stories of the viral overnight sensation who puts up a video of their cat dancing to a weird song, and the next day has a million fans and a six-figure book deal. That *can* happen, but it's about as likely as winning the lottery, meaning you should *not* bet on that. Instead, develop a slow, steady plan for growth. Find something that's working a little bit and keep at it until it's working more and more.

Of course, this means that along the way, you'll likely try things that don't work at all, and it might take a lot of time and effort to even realize that they don't work at all. This is frustrating as hell, but it's part of the process. If you didn't try that thing in the first place, you couldn't rule it out. That doesn't make the process of screaming into the void feel any less annoying, though.

Here are some examples of how I tried things, failed, and reframed my thinking along the way.

The first void I screamed into was the blogging void. I'd heard that being a blogger can help build your author platform, and since books were my primary product, I thought writing a blog would help me reach more customers. My blog wasn't a *total* failure, but it definitely felt like a void.

When I started up my blog in 2017, I wrote 3-5 posts per week. I'd heard all around the internet that *consistency is key*, so I made sure to post at 5 pm every Monday, Wednesday, and Friday, with a few Tuesday or Thursday posts thrown in when I had something extra to say. That way, I'd learned, the Google algorithms would view my website as active and would recommend it higher in search results. Great!

Only problem was… no one was searching for Savy, whom they didn't even know about.

So, I'd spend hours crafting blog posts about a variety of book-related topics: book reviews, updates on my NaNoWriMo progress, writing tips, and business updates. Some of these posts got a couple hundred views! Awesome! I thought I was on a roll. Only thing was… I got no comments.

People may have liked the post enough to click on it, but no one was engaging. Why was this?

I remember writing a post about balancing starting a business with going to grad school. This post took me a couple hours to write, and I even included a cute picture of my "Boss Lady" travel mug. A slam dunk, right?

I thought it was, when I noticed that I had 5 whole comments on this post! Then I started reading the comments. They were things like:

"Do you want to lose 10 pounds in 5 days?"

"Do you want your penis enlarged?"

"Click here for SEO help!"

Yep. It was the bots.

The more comments I got from obvious spam-bots, the less motivated I felt to keep up with my blog. Was it even reaching that many people? Even though writing the posts gave me a chance to practice freewriting, couldn't I be spending that time working on a new book, or on a different marketing platform?

The answer was yes.

Similar to my initial attempts at YouTube, I didn't know how to reach people, and for a long time, I had to scream into the void.

So why was it that when I screamed into the void on Blogger, I got discouraged, but when I screamed into the void on YouTube, I started searching for solutions?

Well, the answer to that is quite simple: I just really like making videos. *Yes!!*

As obvious as it sounds, when you like something, you're going to be more motivated to do it, even if it's not working out the way you want.

I didn't search for solutions about finding a bigger blogging audience because, truth be told, I didn't know a ton about the blogging world or community. I didn't read that many blogs in my spare time unless I was looking for something specific like a recipe. But I *did* watch YouTube. I watched tons of movie critic channels, tons of book review channels, and even a few writing tips channels run by authors. I knew that there was a community I could join, because I already enjoyed consuming the work put out by others in that community.

So, yes, the beginning of my YouTube career was about a year of having *no one* see my videos. But little by little, I learned about communities I could join, key words I could use, and where to find people who enjoyed having discussions with me in the comments of their videos.

Here's another brief tangent, which you can ignore if you're not planning to use YouTube or your business is not book-related. But since I want to give as much specific advice as I can to help you, I would be remiss if I didn't include these tips, just in case it's relevant to what you're doing.

The first video that helped me find a community on YouTube was the BookTube Newbie Tag. If you're joining a community, see if there are any common videos that new members like to make to introduce themselves to that community. I filmed two videos: BookTube Newbie Tag and AuthorTube Newbie Tag. These were a series of questions that I answered to introduce myself to the reading and writing communities on YouTube.

When I started getting comments from people saying, "Welcome to the community!", I would click on their channel, subscribe to it, and leave comments on a few of their videos. Then, I started searching "BookTube Newbie Tag" and "AuthorTube Newbie Tag" on YouTube as well so that I could meet and welcome new members to the community. Next thing I knew, I was making friends on YouTube, and I was starting to grow a small pool of subscribers.

At the time that I'm writing this, I've been consistently posting book and writing related videos for about a year and a half, and I have about 6,000 subscribers on my channel. Not a *massive* following by any means, but one that continues to grow, and one that is open to hearing about my new books.

My best advice in this chapter is this: *know* and *accept* that part of the process is going to be screaming into a void. It's okay to feel frustrated by it. But I just don't want you to feel as blindsided by the void as I did a few years ago. There's a big difference between friends and family reacting to your social media posts, and suddenly selling products on the internet. It's a huge learning curve, or at least it was for me.

While screaming into the void isn't fun, and I can't think of any way to make it fun, the joy comes from finding solutions — to carving out paths within that void that lead you to your target audience.

When you're about to start marketing your business (especially online), and you know that you're about to yell into that void for the first time, here are some questions I'd recommend asking yourself:

- Who is my target customer or audience?
- What social media programs do they use the most?
- How much engagement am I getting on each social media platform?
- Is the engagement I'm getting (likes, views, comments, etc.) growing over time?
- Have I noticed engagement from people other than those I already know in everyday life?
- Is what I'm doing *working* in *any way*?

That last question is key. If it's working in *no way*, as in, not working *at all*, then it might be time to stop and try something new. But if you think there's even the slightest chance it might be working, then it's time to hammer it even harder.

For example:

When I was blogging, my answer to "Is what I'm doing working in any way?" was *yes* at first; I was getting views on my blog. So, I kept writing more posts. But then, if I asked myself the question "Is my engagement growing over time?" the answer was no.

When I started YouTube, my answer to "Is what I'm doing working in any way?" was yes. My first few videos got a few views. After posting my Newbie Tag videos, the answer to "Is my engagement growing over time?" was yes. So, I had to identify what was causing that growth in engagement. Well, posting videos that had "Newbie Tag" in the title was part of it, but I couldn't do that forever. What else was working? Well, searching for *others'* versions of that tag, introducing myself, and working on building a relationship... that was working! It was working *slowly*—I was getting maybe 2 or 3 new subscribers a day from doing that—but it was increasing my engagement, so I continued to do that. The more I continued to do that, the faster the growth became. Suddenly—or rather, slowly but surely—the void began to narrow.

I am not an expert on social media by any means. But what I've learned is that the process of becoming familiar with each community and each platform is slow. It takes a long time to learn how to stand out in the crowd, even just enough to reach a small following.

But the fact that we can even *have* a small following is amazing. The internet has, in a way, blessed us with a certain kind of magic. And that's going to be the topic for our next chapter — the magic of *narrowcasting*.

17

The Magic of Narrowcasting

Someone once asked me, "If you were told *right now* that in 5 minutes, you had to go onstage and give a TED Talk, what would you talk about?"

My answer to this question is, "Wait, I can give a TED Talk? When? Where? I'll do it! Gimme!" In my back pocket, I always have a TED Talk ready to go. I'm constantly chomping at the bit to tell everyone about this concept that's completely revolutionizing the entertainment industry — whether that's movies, music, TV, books, or art — and allowing small businesses to enter formerly gatekept industries.

This is a concept called *narrowcasting*.

As its name would suggest, narrowcasting has become more and more narrow as the internet has gained more prominence in the way people consume media. In my opinion, narrowcasting is one of the best predictors for the future of where certain businesses and industries, especially those involved in entertainment or media, are heading next and how we can prepare for that as entrepreneurs.

So, what is narrowcasting?

Well, we've all heard of broadcasting. We've all seen the way traditional media—like the mainstream TV news, Hollywood movies, etc.— reach a *broad* range of people all at once. Narrowcasting is like broadcasting, but it's also the opposite. What happens when, instead of one giant program trying to hit millions of people at once, millions of small businesses all hit their narrowly defined, target audience of people? Well, if the past few years are anything to go by, the result is that more businesses have a chance to enter the game, and more consumers can find *exactly* what they're looking for. If that sounds confusing, don't worry! I'm going to give lots of examples!

Narrowcasting may be easier to spot in recent years, since the internet has caused the biggest narrowcasting boom since radio. However, the term "narrowcasting" has existed since the 1920s, and it was first coined in a response to local radio programs. While broadcasts spread one message far and wide, local radio signals could send tons of different messages to multiple different locations so each neighborhood, town, or city received the news that was most relevant to them.

The internet has taken this concept and caused it to *explode*.

We've all heard the stories about big, online-based companies causing brick-and-mortar companies to go out of business. Netflix caused the death of Blockbuster. Amazon caused the death of Borders Bookstore. None of this is news to us. But, if we look a little deeper into these examples, we can examine *why* these online companies prevailed while their physical counterparts folded.

Sure, the convenience of being able to shop online from your own home, no longer being forced to brave the elements every time you want to rent a DVD or find a new book, is a huge factor. But there's a lot more than that.

As consumers, we want more than just convenience. We want *options*. When content exists online, there is no cap on how much there can be. There is no limited shelf space on the internet. Anyone can sell anything, which means anyone can *buy* anything. On Amazon, authors don't have to fight for shelf space based on how well their books sell. There are over 30 million books on Amazon, and no one needs to worry about where they're going to store all of them.

Narrowcasting has not only benefited consumers by allowing them to find content that matches their tastes exactly, but it also has allowed new creators to enter the game without having to prove themselves to a company first.

You want to be an actor, but don't want to move to Hollywood and deal with the whole film industry business? Don't worry, I feel the same way. Well, the good news is, you can start a web series and put it up on YouTube, which is gaining more viewers as members of generations Y and Z cut off their cable service.

On YouTube, there are millions of videos uploaded every hour about a variety of topics. People have gotten famous doing everything from makeup tutorials to movie reviews. And you know what? Every single one of these people is a business owner. Every one of these people has a specific audience that consumes their media, and every audience member seeks out that type of content. That could never happen on broadcast television; that's the magic of narrowcasting.

I've personally used two multiple forms of technology born of narrowcasting when starting and growing the Furever Home Friends: YouTube and print-on-demand.

My YouTube channel, SAVY Writes Books, is where I've found a ton of my audience. In fact, while I'm writing this sentence right now, I'm participating in a YouTube livestream with other authors doing NaNoWriMo word sprints. Hi, Lisa and Robert!

In an earlier chapter, we talked about one of my favorite types of narrowcasting: crowdfunding. Before the internet, people couldn't just search through hundreds of up-and-coming businesses that they might want to support. Sure, you could support a small business by shopping at the locally owned corner store instead of the Walmart. And that's great! But what if that locally owned corner store was struggling to get the money to pay their first month's rent deposit and could have sold some of their products online in a crowdfunding campaign?

One of the many things I love about crowdfunding is how it allows a specific crowd to connect with a specific creator who's making exactly what they're looking for and want to support. If I want to browse new comic books in the works, I can go on Kickstarter and filter my results to find exactly that. Similarly, if I want to find indie lesbian romance, I can search for that on Amazon.

Now, the main difference between *broadcasting* and *narrowcasting* is that none of these creators (myself included!) are likely to ever have a broad audience. That indie lesbian romance author will probably never sell as much as JK Rowling or

Stephen King. But she absolutely can make a respectable full-time income with a core audience.

Similarly, my own business, the Furever Home Friends, is not as big or nationally recognized as a company like American Girl or Build-a-Bear. But that's *okay*. I'm a *small business owner*. My goal was to create products, put them into the world, and make enough money to sustain my own life while doing that. My goal was never to be a wealthy, powerful, billionaire CEO. There are already enough business books out there if you're pursuing that. In this book, we love small businesses and target audiences!

I love that we live in an age when our favorite musicians, actors, writers, and creators can be people that our friends may have never heard of. That's not just the hipster in me talking—okay, I guess the hipster in me is *always* talking; they've been talking since before it was cool—but I love how the creative world is no longer a zero-sum game. It's not all-or-nothing anymore. You can be successful and work in a creative field full-time without becoming super famous or wealthy. You no longer have to choose between starving actor waiting tables and Hollywood mega-star; right now, there is so much in the middle of the spectrum.

One of my favorite examples of narrowcasting is my favorite band of all time. Many people who have seen me on YouTube like to assume that my favorite band is Nirvana or the Red Hot Chili Peppers or something (probably because I dress like a 90s bitch), but the truth is, my favorite band is—you guessed it!—also a small business.

Every time they are in Chicago, come hell or high water, I *am* going to see Planet Booty in concert. Planet Booty is a three-person band producing electro-funk music with body-positive lyrics about the worship of the ass. What more could I want? I'm a full-on stan of this band. I have had all the members of Planet Booty sign my butt at a concert. I considered getting their signatures tattooed on my butt, but currently don't have the budget for three new tattoos. For Christmas, Tyler made me my own Planet Booty shrine out of a butt mannequin, which he covered in metallic disco-ball sequins, and displayed a pair of booty shorts that all the band members have signed.

So, why am I gushing about Planet Booty right now? Is it because I'm drunk on bourbon and they're LITERALLY ACTUALLY THE BEST BAND OF ALL TIME?!

Yes.

But that's not the only reason. It's also because their success, and the reason I was able to find them in the first place, was all the result of narrowcasting.

I first heard of Planet Booty when I went to a TWRP concert. TWRP is a band whose original name was Tupperware Remix Party, but then they got in trouble with Tupperware over copyright stuff, so now they're just TWRP. I wanted to see TWRP because I thought it was hilarious that their band had a multilevel marketing company in their name. Tyler wanted to see TWRP because he actually liked their music.

Tyler had first heard of TWRP because they often toured with a band he liked called Ninja Sex Party. Ninja Sex Party first gained their following through their YouTube channel, which has been active for over ten years. Ninja Sex Party really blew up when their lead singer became a co-host on the multimillion-subscriber YouTube channel The Game Grumps.

So, let's review: a gaming YouTube channel, which is already a form of narrowcasting, caused a band to take off. That band touring with another band helped that second band gain a following, which is how my spouse first learned of them. That second band then toured with a *third* band, whom I saw in concert because I tagged along with Tyler, and now that third band, Planet Booty, is my favorite band of all time.

Literally *every* step of this process was narrowcasting in action. And it was all *indie as hell*. Never once did a massive record label or music corporation need to get involved.

Statistically speaking, you likely haven't heard of Planet Booty, unless you read my Twitter feed regularly. But now you have. And that's the magic of narrowcasting!

Narrowcasting has been a huge part of my philosophy as a business owner ever since I decided to treat my writing as its own business rather than in the traditional way. For those of you who aren't super immersed in the book world, the traditional way to become an author (though trends are now changing — largely due to internet-induced narrowcasting) is to pitch your manuscript to a bunch of literary agents, find an agent to sign with, have that agent pitch your book to a bunch of publishers, then negotiate a book deal for the publisher to buy the rights, and *then* your book begins the publication process.

In this process, you would be the author — one role out of a larger machine, rather than the CEO. Let me be clear: there is *nothing* wrong with that! I'm actually pursuing the traditional publishing process with a couple of my own books. But for Furever Home Friends, I didn't want to fill a strict role of "author." As I mentioned toward the beginning of this book, from the company's initial conception, I had a full model in mind for how I wanted it to run. Because of that, I wasn't going to put books into the world in the traditional way.

What did that mean for me? Well, it DID put me at a few disadvantages from the start. Without a traditional publisher, I had to FUND the process myself, including illustration, marketing, and book printing. We talked all about how I accomplished that in the Crowdfunding chapter. The other main disadvantage was that I had to find my own audience. With a large publishing corporation, you might get assigned a publicist, or at the very least, your publisher will be distributing your book to stores for you and helping it find customers through those avenues.

When you own a business and no one knows who you are, who is going to care that you put out a new product? Let alone care *enough* to open up their wallet for you? That's why I needed to build my author platform—which is just a fancy way of saying I connected with my target audience.

As an independent creator and a small business owner, that platform came through narrowcasting. I didn't go into this planning to have my books fly off the shelves like *Harry Potter*, or to have my plushies instantly line the toy aisles of big-box retailers next to Mattel toys. Instead, I planned to find a small audience who would want my products. I didn't go into this to become a millionaire—I went into this to become a self-sustaining small business owner, and nothing more.

As we discussed in the previous chapter, a main avenue for narrowcasting to my audience is my YouTube channel. YouTube is a wonderful form of narrowcasting; it allows small video creators and up-and-coming filmmakers to cultivate a dedicated audience without needing the backing of a big TV studio. Many of my current customers found me through my YouTube channel, through my Facebook group for women in business, or through my involvement with local animal shelters both in person and online.

So, how might you use the principle of narrowcasting to find your target customers? Well, if you're like me, you might want to start a YouTube channel. Small business ownership on YouTube can be really fun; you can create vlogs showing your potential customers behind-the-scenes looks and how you create your products or what a day in your life looks like. You might also use Instagram for a similar purpose.

Try to brainstorm all the elements of your business and see if you can find a community online who enjoys those elements. For example, if you want to start releasing indie music, maybe find some music reaction channels on YouTube, comment on their videos, and make a few of your own before announcing your original music. If you create homemade cosmetic products, maybe find some smaller beauty gurus on YouTube or beauty influencers on Instagram. Connect with them, comment on their posts, and start to see who follows you back. Start posting some content of your own to generate buzz.

The beauty of narrowcasting is that every subculture has its own community on the internet nowadays. I can idolize someone as a celebrity, but my best friends could have no idea who that person is. *You* can become someone that a small group of people idolize—or, your business can!

Basically, narrowcasting is the perfect model for a small business. You don't *need* to grow, expand, and explode—we talked about that in the "To Scale or Not to Scale?" chapter. What's crucial is finding the specific people who need what you have to offer.

Go find that community. Go find that subculture. Go find the group of people on Instagram who like to take pictures of their plushies traveling around the world pretending to be on vacation. (Yep—this is a subculture, and I've used a lot of their hashtags to notify them about the Furever Home Friends plushies!) The right community for you *is* out there. Start casting to them!

#SAVVYBUSINESSOWNER

Part 5

The Myths of Boss Babe Life

18

The Myth: Hard Work is All You Need
The Truth: Hard Work Isn't Always Enough

I'm almost hesitant to talk about the L word here, luck, because it's opening up a dangerous rabbit hole. The mere concept of *luck* can be a major deterrent to many potential entrepreneurs.

Knowing that luck exists can cause people to think, "Well, if my business failed, it was just bad luck," or, "If I'm not doing as well as my competitors, it's because they're luckier than I am." This *can* be true. But no one should *rely* on luck as an explanation. In the upcoming paragraphs, I'm hoping to reframe the way you think about luck as a concept.

We all love a good underdog story. Here, I'll tell one about myself: Savy was born to a low-income single mother from the Polish South Side of Chicago. Savy started up a business, the Furever Home Friends, bought a home at age 23, and lives a successful life as a full-time writer.

Great story, yeah? It's technically true, too. None of that is factually incorrect. But it *is* misleading. There were a *lot* of other things that happened in between that made each of those things possible, and some of it was pure dumb luck.

A lot of my fellow millennials are probably still hung up on the whole "bought a home at 23" thing. Yeah, I did that. Some people say I should tout that as an accomplishment. But it's not. It was *luck*.

Here's the part where I get super, *super* honest and transparent with you all. I think a lot of the time, business owners neglect their own privilege in favor of sounding like they did it all themselves. That's an understandable tactic; after all, who's going to take business advice from someone who says, "Yeah, I was born rich." Now their success doesn't sound attainable anymore!

Well, if it helps at all, I wasn't born rich. But I did marry rich. And I'm not going to lie about that. I also didn't stay in a single-parent household forever. My mom eventually married a wonderful man who adopted me and became my father, and I'm grateful every day to have had his guidance in

This is fascinating & true!!

my life. My mom didn't marry rich, but she did marry us out of poverty.

(Actually—forgive my brief tangent here—this phenomenon is something I'd like to see studied more from a sociological perspective. We never hear much about kids who come from mixed-income backgrounds. My childhood was pretty much divided into two halves: I started with a single mom who worked four jobs and lived below the poverty line, and I finished high school in a two-parent household in a suburban, upper-middle-class community. It's very *weird* to have come from both of those backgrounds equally, and maybe I'll write more about this experience in the future. Basically, it's a string of feeling like you don't quite belong anywhere; you don't fit in with the rich kids at school because there's something *off* about you that screams "I came from a poor family," but you also don't fit in with your other poor friends, because you had ridiculous levels of privilege that they didn't. It's weird.)

Now, when I say I married rich, that's a bit of an exaggeration. I was being dramatic, I admit it. I didn't find a sugar daddy. Trust me, I'm not pretty enough for that.

As you all know, I'm married to Tyler. He's a great guy. And his family getting rich was, for me, *luck*. I met Tyler when I was 11 years old. We were in the same sixth-grade homeroom, and we were best friends throughout middle school. We went on our first date at 14, dated on and off until we were 22, and then bought a home together at 23. When my eleven-year-old ass first met Tyler, I had no way to know that, 10 years in the future, his parents would get offered a job opportunity in China that would make them a metric butt-load of money. But they did. And they were then in a position to loan us a significant chunk of money for a down payment on our first home, an apartment in Chicago. For me, all of that was *luck*.

Me starting my own business was *not* luck. That was hard work, 90-hour weeks, finely honed time management skills, and more. But it sure was helpful that I already had a home while I was starting this business.

So, where am I going with this? I think a lot of business owners are hesitant to mention the L word, luck, or the P word, privilege, for fear that it will alienate their audiences. No one wants their readers to think, "Well, I don't know any rich people, so I'm just fucked." I've had a harder time than someone who was born into the entertainment industry or someone who comes from a family of business owners. But I've had a much easier time than someone living without a home. The fact is, in all of our lives, we have our own sets of advantages and disadvantages, and it's up to each of us to figure out how to best use the bits of luck we *do* have to our benefit. We're all the underdog in the story when we compare ourselves to someone who started off wealthier or who had more connections in our industry. But we're also the villain in someone else's story.

We all have to harness our own unique blend of hard work and luck to make a business successful. Many other authors focus on the *hard work* part, since it's the only part that we really have any control over. But using our own circumstances to our advantage, and recognizing that we each have an advantage that someone else may not, can also help us see the world — and ourselves — more clearly.

Plus, once we've identified those advantages, we can figure out ways to help level the playing field for those who don't have them. If your advantage is simply that you have a roof over your head, you can look for small businesses to support that employ homeless people. Or *you* can help break that barrier by not requiring people to list a physical address when applying to work for your business. If one of your advantages is that you went to college, you can seek employees based solely on their portfolio without even asking about their degrees. (Unless you're entering a field that requires specific licensure, of course.)

Basically, what I'm saying is, recognize which advantages you've had in life and which you haven't. Don't assume that those who don't reach your success are struggling due to a lower work ethic or lack of skill. And don't assume that when someone is doing *better* than you that it's solely because they *are* better.

But don't forget: you still do have to work really, really hard. So get ready for that part—it's time for the law of *action*!

19

The Myth: Law of Attraction?
The Truth: More Like, Law of ACTION!

Ready for me to trash some other business books I've read? Ready for me to talk about how much better I am than those *other business writers?* Get ready for some serious not-like-other-girls energy! I'm not like other bossbabes, and I'm here to let you all know it!

Honestly, a lot of you probably found me on YouTube through my reviews trashing other books, so you'll be excited to hear me complain now.

Side note: I'm well aware that means I'm opening myself up for a *butt-load* of criticism when this book comes out. With the number of self-help and business books I've publicly trashed on

YouTube, I'm *so ready* for the negative reviews to come rolling my way and for me to get hit with that sweet karma.

One of the things that annoys me most in business books and self-help books is how much the authors attribute their success to the law of attraction. Now, to be fair, the law of attraction isn't *complete* BS; I'd say it's half BS and half placebo effect. That placebo-effect half *can* make it all worthwhile.

The *law of attraction* states that if you think positive thoughts and put positive ideas out into the world, good things will happen to you. It theorizes that you'll become a positivity magnet, using your own optimism to attract success. Now, that sounds like BS, right? That's because it is.

I used to get really frustrated when I'd crack open a business book looking for advice on marketing or scaling, and instead would find chapters upon chapters of these wildly successful entrepreneurs telling me how they used the law of attraction to achieve success. I didn't want to hear how asking the universe for something made it magically appear, or how putting positive thoughts out into the world caused positive circumstances to manifest themselves.

When other books would tell me this, I'd feel torn. On the one hand, there was no way that made logical sense. I could think, "I'm going to sell a thousand books today!" all I wanted, but at the end of the day, that wasn't going to make it happen.

If the law of attraction really worked like some of these entrepreneurs said it did, then why were there people dying every day due to unforeseen circumstances? Why were some people randomly hit by natural disasters? And, on a smaller scale, why did some people's businesses fail, despite years of hard work and positive thinking? To me, the law of attraction felt like victim-blaming.

On the other hand, though, these people telling me about the law of attraction were successful. They'd built businesses that made them wealthy, and they made a full-time income doing what they loved. So there had to be *something* to this, right?

I pondered this over many rides on Chicago public transportation, long after reading these books had caused me motion sickness on the bus. I'd put down the books, and I'd ponder. Well, friends, I think I figured it out:

The law of attraction is really the law of *action*.

It's not that these other entrepreneurial authors were lying to me; it's just that they weren't telling the whole story. Whether that's intentional or not, I'll never know; I'm not a mind reader.

The law of attraction *itself* didn't bring these people success; the *action* they followed their positive thoughts up with did.

For example, one business book I read told the story of a female business owner. Let's call her Barbara. That's not her real name. Barbara said that, when she put ideas out into the universe and believed in their possibility, those things would always come true for her. She explained that, in one case, she used the visualization technique. She imagined herself winning an award at an upcoming pitch competition she was attending. She visualized the way the room would look when she's onstage, the way the crowd would sound, and the feeling of the environment around her. She imagined herself speaking, giving her pitch. And then she imagined the feeling of receiving her award at the end. And wouldn't you know it, Barbara *did* end up winning the award!

So, what caused Barbara to win the award? Putting the idea into the universe that she would? Thinking only positive thoughts? No. *Confidence*.

Here's my theory on why Barbara actually won this award. By visualizing the event in such great detail, she forced herself to practice her presentation over and over. By believing that positive thinking would help her, she armed herself with confidence. Then, when she took the stage, she eloquently delivered a well-practiced pitch. In other words, she followed up her optimism with *action*.

There's nothing wrong with staying positive. Hell, barely a second goes by that I'm *not* smiling. I'm loud, I'm obnoxious, and I'm told that I exude excitement. But these attributes alone do not make me a successful business owner. It's the way I *use* these qualities to reach customers.

Having a positive outlook doesn't bring customers to my table. *Using* my positive outlook to fearlessly call people over with a friendly smile, genuinely excited to meet them, *that* is what brings customers to my table.

Visualizing myself winning grant money doesn't make the money appear. But walking onto a stage to deliver a pitch I practiced over and over again, confident that I know what I'm doing because I practiced it both in my head *and* in front of the mirror, *that's* what helps me win grant money.

Reframing how we look at positive thinking is important for identifying your next steps as a business owner. At least, it was for me. Because here's the problem: if we spend too much time worried about having a positive outlook, we might end up in a thought spiral. (Or, at least, I would, but that might be because I have OCD, which causes me to fall into intrusive thought spirals all the time.) For me, focusing too much on positive thinking goes like this:

"I didn't win this award/make this sale/hit my goals this month. That's okay! I must've not been thinking positive enough! Now it's time to think EVEN MORE POSITIVE! I can do it! This month is going to be even better! Yeah! Time to hustle!"

Then, when the next month, the same thing happens, it becomes harder and harder to just "stay positive" with no tangible results. This leads to a cycle of what some people are now calling "toxic positivity." I completely agree with that name for the phenomenon. We get so tied up in having to think positive all the time that we don't allow ourselves to feel our full range of emotions. We don't allow ourselves to be sad, identify what's making us sad, and then try to brainstorm solutions. To me, toxic positivity is about smiling through the pain, rather than admitting you're hurting and searching for a solution.

Instead, here's how I might approach a month where I didn't meet my goals:

"Okay, so I didn't hit my sales goals for this month. Where was I lacking? Well, I hit my goal at this event, but I didn't make as many website sales as I wanted. I had a discount code running for a weekend, but only 1 person used it, so maybe my audience isn't motivated by a 25% off coupon. Maybe they are motivated by something else, like a limited-time product. Let's try that instead."

In a way, I'm still thinking positive--I'm believing that the solution *is out there*, even if I haven't found it yet, but I'm also admitting that I failed. Failure doesn't mean that it's over; it just means it's time to look at the situation in a new way.

But failure is *going* to happen. And it's *okay* to feel sad when it does—as long as the next day, you use that sadness as fuel for your next brainstorming session.

20

The Myth: Entrepreneurship Gives You the Financial Freedom to Be Home
The Truth: You Will Not See Your Family More Often

I don't like to be abusive to my books. As an author, I love and value books and want to keep them safe on my shelf. But I almost threw a business book at the damn *wall* when I read an author telling me that "some people start businesses because they want to see their families more often" and acting like that was a valid reason.

But Savy, I do want to see my family more often! I thought if I started my own business and became self-employed, I could spend more time with my spouse/kids/dog/whoever. In my experience, that's been a straight-up lie. The idea that self-employment will make you *more* available to your family is, at best, a lie other entrepreneurs sell you so you'll buy their books and courses. If my experience is anything to go by, you'll not only *not* see your family more, but it will be a struggle to see your family and friends at all.

Don't let that discourage you, though. Here's my usual, bright-letters-flashing-across-the-screen disclaimer for you: *this is only my experience.* Maybe some other business owners have found ways to make running a business take *fewer* hours than working a regular full-time job. Maybe they also have a pet unicorn who farts rainbows. Maybe that pet unicorn also has a property in Iowa you'd be interested in.

On average, business owners work about 60 hours a week. In the US, the average full-time employee works 40 hours a week; meaning business owners take on *one and a half* full-time workloads. And 60 hours a week is just the average; honestly, if your business is new, there's a good chance you'll end up working 80, 90, or 100 hours a week like I did back when I was in school.

But Savy, my business allows me to work from home! I do freelance graphic design/copyediting/custom art/anything that isn't a pyramid scheme, and I can do it all from my living room. That's great, and I think that's what a lot of other business authors are getting at

257

when they say you can see your family more often; I think what they really mean is, you can be in the same physical location as your family more often. Sometimes.

When I first started the Furever Home Friends, Tyler was lucky if he could have dinner with me once a week. I was in awe of people who somehow ran a business and/or went to school *while having kids*. How did their kids stay alive? How did they find the money for a nanny? What was going on?

Here's what I'm getting at with all of this: don't go into a business venture *expecting* more time with your family and friends. Just because you're now in charge of your own schedule *does not mean* that you have more free time. You actually have less free time and more tasks to complete: you're just the one who gets to decide how you structure it.

I realize that this chapter is probably depressing as hell so far.

But Savy, you're probably asking. *Why are you writing a chapter about how I'm going to struggle to see my family and friends? Why are you trying to bring me down? How is this depressing-ass chapter supposed to help me?*

Well, I could say the obvious answer: it's going to help you have a realistic expectation of what business owner life is like.

But beyond that, I think understanding this concept can really help with another thing: time management.

I'm sure it's obvious that time management is *crucial* when you're trying to run a business. Not only do you have to be ridiculously self-motivated and disciplined, but for many of us, at the start, we also have to juggle day jobs until the business starts turning a profit.

So here are some of my best tips for managing your time and still finding ways to prioritize the important people and relationships in your life. I won't lie to you and say it's easy to have recreational time, but you can absolutely make it all work.

Back in the goal-setting chapter, I discussed how I use different planners to map out different goals. Planners, for me, are also necessary to manage my time and make sure not only everything gets done, but also that the people in my life don't think I've disappeared. (I have had that happen before. In the past, there have been times when I've done a crappy job at balancing everything and have gone months without seeing family or friends.)

This might sound silly, but *schedule* your non-work-related items! *Schedule* your time with your friends, your family, your significant other. Every single day in my daily/weekly planner, I write "dinner with Tyler" in the evening slots. It's important to me that we have dinner together and use some of that time to play with Chewie. Back when I was juggling all of this *while* in grad school, I was never home for dinner. I was in night class. It sucked never being able to schedule time to see people in my life—so when the option is there, schedule it. Make it a priority.

I also schedule my personal care habits, like eating and showering. If I don't write "lunch" and "shower" in my planner every day, and block it out in yellow on my Google calendar, I *will* forget to do it, and I *will* sit up at night wondering why I'm so hungry and why I smell so bad.

While I highly recommend blocking out time for these necessities, you also have to figure out how to best manage your time getting your actual work tasks completed. I'm not the expert in this—I'm typing this sentence at 1:20 in the morning while I have a jam-packed Monday tomorrow.

Every week, I schedule blocks of time to *work*. Schedule a lot of them, and schedule more than you need.

I often schedule a few blocks of time at night, after I've had dinner with Tyler and played with Chewie, just in case I couldn't finish everything during the day. (As you can probably tell by the fact that I'm writing this at 1:20 in the morning, those extra blocks were necessary this week.)

When scheduling, be *specific*. Don't just say "from 9am-1pm, work on my business." Instead, say:

- 9 am: package up this week's orders
- 10 am: ship out orders at the post office
- 11 am: eat lunch; while eating, watch 10 YouTube videos of people in my target audience, comment on those videos, and plan reach outs
- 12 pm: work on revisions to newest draft of book (or whatever the equivalent is in your field)

The more specific you are, the easier it will be to manage your time. We already talked about making daily goals and to-do lists in the Goal-Setting chapter, but I'm reiterating it here because of the importance of managing your time.

Work efficiently, work intentionally, and work a lot. But don't forget to schedule time for both self-care and for the care of others in your life. You've got this!

21

The Myth: The Customer is Always Right
The Truth: Sometimes the Customer SUCKS!

Despite this being the last chapter of this book, I'm going to dive into a topic that could probably fill *another* entire book with anecdotes.

When you run a small business, some people can be straight-up *rude* to you. These instances are fun for me to rant about on Twitter, but in the moment, they can feel heartbreaking. In these cases, I like to remember that one of the most famous business aphorisms of all time, "The customer is always right," is a myth.

Before I delve into the reasons *why* this is a myth, let's enjoy some anecdotes.

One time, I was selling my Furever Home Friends books and plushies at an art fair in Chicago. I had painstakingly set up my 10-foot tent outside on a cold morning at the beginning of the midwestern autumn, fighting through gusts that prove *windy city* is more than a moniker, and arranged an adorable dog-themed fall display.

On one table, my plush dogs sat roasting dog-sized marshmallows together over a dog-sized campfire. Next to them, other stuffed animals rode a dog-sized hayride across the table. On a different table, I set up some coloring pages, full of black-and-white versions of the books' illustrations, for the kids that came into the tent, along with a set of colored pencils they could use.

Most people loved this display, and my sales were great this weekend. But you know what wasn't great? The one random, full-grown adult woman who came up to my coloring-page table, picked up a colored pencil off of the table, stuck it down the back of her shirt and scratched her back with it, and then put it back in the pile. *What the…?*

Another time, at one of my first holiday-themed events of the year, I had my big "Happy Pawlidays" display set up, and a large group of people in front of my table. It's difficult to engage a lot of customers at once, especially when you want to talk to everyone about your products one-on-one.

One lady had me fully locked in conversation; she was telling me all about her adorable cat and showing me pictures of him on her phone. That's great!

It's often that people will see my table, recognize me as an animal person, and start up a conversation about their own pets. This can be really fun; connecting with other dog (or cat!) people is the best. Sometimes, people will ask me, "Can you do a book about my pet?" My answer is always that I have the next couple characters planned out already, but will definitely be open to suggestions in the future (which is the truth).

I was enjoying seeing pictures of this lady's cat, but we had been in conversation for about ten minutes, and I also had a few other people at the table that I needed to talk to. I said, "Hey, your cat is adorable! I'm going to tell these people about the products really quick, but feel free to look through the books in the meantime!"

Her response? "Oh, I'm not a customer."

I think people don't always realize how, as a small business owner, *this is my workday*. This is how I make my living. While I love having conversations and getting to know every potential customer, I unfortunately do not have time to have twenty-minute conversations with every single person who doesn't intend to buy. I wish I did; as an extrovert, it kills me! But that's the hard truth, and sometimes it saddens me that people outside of the small business world don't realize that what we're doing is our jobs.

When something like this happens, I always have to resist the urge to blurt out something like: "I don't come to *your* office during the workday and sit on *your desk* while you're trying to reach customers and just tell you all about Chewie for an hour, now do I?" Though, come to think of it, maybe I *should* start barging into people's offices to show them pictures of Chewie.

Out of all these stories, though, this one takes the cake. I was selling my products at a holiday craft bazaar held inside a community center in one of the Chicago suburbs. This community center included a gym, so a lot of people passing by had just come from their workouts. Some people were carrying gym bags, some were holding yoga mats, some were in workout clothes, and some were carrying their sneakers in their hands, since their feet were now covered in boots, ready to venture back out into the snowy Chicago winter. hell no b b

As people passed by my table, some stopped to discuss the products, get a signed book, or buy a plush. Some stopped to say hi. This one lady, who was carrying her sneakers, stopped right in front of my table, and appeared to be looking at my products. I was about to greet her, when suddenly I noticed what she was doing.

She was stopping briefly to arrange her gym bag, and in the process, she had *set her sneakers down on my table*. Before I could say anything, she picked them back up and continued on her way. I was grateful that my mom was off talking with a different customer at the time; she's *very* into cleanliness and would've had a heart attack right then and there.

As a small business owner, you might get some serious disrespect from random-ass people. These people are not right to do this.

So I guess the saying shouldn't be, "The customer is always right." It should be, "The customer is always the customer." Or, "The customer always holds power." In a sales situation, you're trying to get someone to part with their hard-earned money. That's not easy, regardless of how good your product is.

Nothing Sells Itself

Have you ever heard the phrase "it sells itself?" Just like "the customer is always right," this is another myth!

Way back in Chapter 3, we discussed MLMs and pyramid schemes; these are often the companies trying to convince someone that a product "sells itself"; that sales doesn't really require any work if a product is good enough or unique enough. This is false.

I don't care if you've discovered a magical potion that can cure any disease at the drop of a hat and you're selling it for under a dollar. *Nothing* sells itself. Even the biggest, most well-known, most successful companies out there—places like Amazon, Coca-Cola, Google, and more—still have sales and marketing departments. The hard truth is, sales is *difficult*, and no matter how good your product is, sales is *work*.

Sometimes the Customer is Objectively WRONG; But at the End of the Day, You Have to Sell

At that same holiday bazaar where a lady put her shoes on my table (gross), another approached my table and stared at my products. After a moment, she poked one of my plush dog's eyes, turned to me, and said, "This isn't safe."

"What?" I asked.

"This is a choking hazard," she replied.

As a human, I had the instinct to yell, "Hey lady, if your kids are trying to eat the safely secured eyes out of their stuffed animals, that's *your* problem!"

But as a business owner, I knew that I needed to be polite. The truth is, the customer can be objectively wrong like she was—but that's an opportunity to correct the customer in *favor* of a sale.

"Actually, they're very safe!" I told her. "The manufacturer certified that these plushies are safe for children to handle. All materials used have been approved and they've been sewn together securely." Then, I showed her the tag sticking out of plush Chewie's butt, which detailed the ways the toys are safe for kids.

I don't think she ended up buying one, but hey, that customer just sucked. Some customers are going to suck. But that's a great opportunity for you to practice how you present information to them.

Because at the end of the day, as cliché as it sounds, the customer is the customer. Even though the customer isn't always right, the customer always has the money. By all means, correct a customer when they have a misconception, especially if that misconception might prevent them from buying. But always remember that they hold the money.

Even if they put their shoes where they shouldn't scratch their back with your art supplies, and can't stop their rabid kids from eating every plastic toy that comes their way.

CONCLUSION

I started writing this book for NaNoWriMo in 2019. Today' it's July 22, 2020, and I'm finishing up the edits to the manuscript. I'm getting ready to prepare ARCs for my wonderful street team and advance reviewers. I'm getting ready to launch this book on my 28th birthday, September 8, just liked I predicted I would in my Goal Setting chapter.

Over the past 8 months, the world has changed in many ways that impact small business owners. I never predicted how many things I'd have to add or change to address the ways I shifted my goals and visions with the COVID19 pandemic hit. As scary as that was, it was a brutal reminder that the world of business ownership is about constant adaptation.

I hope this book taught you something new about starting a business, whether that's some new ideas for raising money to start one, or a new method of goal setting and planning to try. And if you were one of those people who hated networking and public speaking, I really, *really* hope I helped you see it in a new way.

As I mentioned in the beginning of the book, I am open to hearing back from all of you. I want to hear how this book impacted you. If you loved this book, tell me! Leave me a review! If you hated this book, tell me that as well — if you're planning to start a business and you felt that I didn't tell you enough, I want to be there for you to help more. Slide into my DMs. Email me. I'm now a part of *your* expanding network!

I promised myself when I started this book that there would be no cheesy lines or clichés in this, but hey, in the world of disruptive business, rules are meant to be broken. So here's the last thought I'll leave you with:

Turn your passion into a profession. Turn your creativity into a career. And when you approach business, don't forget to be savvy.

ACKNOWLEDGMENTS

First, I need to shout out every Furever Home Friends employee. Thank you to Christy Schneyman, illustrator of *Smile, Chewie!*, Brenda Clemente, illustrator of *Princess Allee*, and Jan Spivey Gilchrist, illustrator of *Kringle's Christmas*, all of whom have done a beautiful job bringing our furry friends to life on the page. Thank you to RK Gold, our social media manager, who helped us create a strong footprint in the social media world. Of course, this is where I normally *would* also shout out Lola Leiser, our stuffed animal designer; but Mom, you're getting a whole paragraph at the end!

Second, a major thank-you to everyone who has supported me on Patreon at any point since I began my YouTube channel. At the time of my writing this, here are the people who currently are or have been Patreon supporters. (If you joined my Patreon after I completed this book, I apologize for not having you in here!) Thank you to Patty Nolan, Ilyana Banana, Jacey Lofton, Zacary Ryan, Shonda Belknap, Kat Benson, Victoria Page, Alyssa, Amanda Mc, Sophia Stafford, Kristine Petersone, Zenita Dee, Judy Van Cleef, Emily Grimm, Alane

Fideler, Maggie K, RK Gold, Markus Regius, Andreana Bitsis, BC Brown, Em Catlett, Krysta D, nivixious, Tess, Eva Writes, Emilee A, Dana Gaulin, and Rue Lew.

Third, I want to shout out my *amazing* street team! You all helped me promote this book for months before its release and I appreciate everything you've done to get this book out there. Shout-out to Dal Cecil Runo, Crystal Rickard, Hiroshi Simizu, Barbara Howard, Jessica Sayers, Danielle Mamaril, and BC Brown.

Thank you to my sisters in the anti-MLM community, Monica Siembieda and Taylor Leigh, for collaborating with me on YouTube and teaming up with me to help spread the word against multilevel marketing companies and in favor of real small businesses.

I also want to recognize my fellow writers who collaborated on livestreams with me as I wrote this. As many of my YouTube followers might know, I wrote the majority of this book during writing sprints on AuthorTube livestreams. A special thank you to Lisa Daily for hosting the Wednesday morning livestream where I would often make the biggest strides in progressing on this book.

And thank you to my Wednesday night AuthorTube Sleepover friends; as we speak, I'm writing this acknowledgments page on a stream with y'all! Thank you to Lauren Sevier, Dal Cecil Runo, BC Brown, RK Gold, Lisa Daily, Samantha Nasset, CB Ferrenz, and Sako Tumi.

I also want to thank everyone who read any part of this book and gave me feedback during my early stages of writing. Specifically, thank you to Jennifer Finstrom from the DePaul Writing Center, and thank you to my critique group friends, Emily, Nancy, Amy, Rebecca, Leah, and Malayna. I know I haven't been present in the group lately because of how much I've been juggling, but I cannot express enough how much I appreciate your support!

Thank you to my husband, partner, and best friend *literally* forever, Tyler. You've not only supported me emotionally, but also supported my business. For every event or festival where I needed help setting up a major display, you were there for me. For every book signing where Chewie made a guest appearance and you gave him treats to make sure he behaved, *thank you.* For every Pawlidays party where I needed your help running credit cards, you never let me down. Your support for me and my overly ambitious career is something I'm grateful for every day of my life. I love you.

Finally, the biggest thank-you of all to the one person who made *not only* this book, but also the entire Furever Home Friends business, possible: my mom, Dolores Leiser, or Lola. Thank you for believing in my crazy ideas from the beginning. Thank you for saying, "Yes!" when I asked you to go into business with me. Thank you for designing the most adorable, snuggly, friendly, lifelong plushie friends I could imagine. And thank you for telling me to write a story about Allee way back in the day, nearly 15 years ago, which inspired me to start this business in the first place. I can't wait to travel to more events with you when the quarantine is over. Thank you for sharing your professional expertise as an event planner to make our displays stand out from the crowd. Thank you for spending days on end working on new plushie designs, new accessory designs, and new display ideas with me. This business is as much yours as it is mine.

ABOUT THE AUTHOR

SAVY is a Chicago author, artist, video creator, and small business owner. SAVY founded the Furever Home Friends in 2017 and has now won several awards as an author and business owner. In 2018, Furever Home Friends was named one of the Top 4 Most Purposeful Startups in Chicago by the Coleman Entrepreneurship Center & 1871. Also the author of *Sculpt Yourself, One Final Vinyl,* and *Beauty King,* SAVY writes young adult and new-adult fiction focused on mental health issues and the LGBTQ+ community.

You can find SAVY on the YouTube channel SAVY Writes Books and on Instagram & Twitter at @savyleiser.

Made in United States
North Haven, CT
06 July 2022

21024844R00168